[WORLD PR
AN ABBEY THEATRE

D1189959

ABBEY THEATRE
NO ROMANCE
NANCY HARRIS

Premiered by the Abbey Theatre
on the Peacock stage on 1 March 2011.

The Abbey Theatre gratefully acknowledges the financial
support of the Arts Council / An Chomhairle Ealaíon.

The play is set in Ireland in the present.

There will be one interval of 15 minutes

CAST (*in order of appearance*)

Laura	Janet Moran
Gail	Natalie Radmall-Quirke
Carmel	Tina Kellegher
Joe	Stephen Brennan
Peg	Stella McCusker
Michael	Conor Mullen
Johnny	Dáire Cassidy

Director	Wayne Jordan
Set and Lighting Design	Paul Keogan
Costume Design	Donna Geraghty
Music and Sound Design	Carl Kennedy
Video Design	Rachel Sullivan
Company Stage Manager	Anne Kyle
Deputy Stage Manager	Stephen Dempsey
Assistant Stage Manager	Orla Burke
Voice Director	Andrea Ainsworth
Casting Director	Holly Ní Chiardha (CDG)
Hair and Make-up	Val Sherlock
Chaperone	Emma Ryan
Photography	Ros Kavanagh
Graphic Design	Zero-G
Sign Language Interpreter	Ali Stewart

ABBEY THEATRE
NO ROMANCE
NANCY HARRIS

No Romance by Nancy Harris is an Abbey Theatre commission.

No Romance is part of our published playscript series.
For further titles in the series please visit www.abbeytheatre.ie

Please note that the text which appears in this volume may be changed during the
rehearsal process and appear in a slightly altered form in performance.

Special thanks to the Betty Ann Norton Theatre School
and the Irish Cancer Society.

. . .

ABBEY THEATRE
Amharclann na Mainistreach

The Abbey Theatre, Ireland's national theatre was founded by W.B. Yeats and Lady Gregory in 1904 to 'bring upon the stage the deeper thoughts and emotions of Ireland'. Since it first opened its doors, the Abbey Theatre has played a vital and often controversial role in the literary, social and cultural life of Ireland.

Over the years, the Abbey Theatre has nurtured and premiered the work of major playwrights such as J.M. Synge and Sean O'Casey as well as contemporary classics from the likes of Sebastian Barry, Marina Carr, Bernard Farrell, Brian Friel, Frank McGuinness, Thomas Kilroy, Tom Mac Intyre, Tom Murphy, Mark O'Rowe, Billy Roche and Sam Shepard. We continue to support new Irish writing at the Abbey through our commissioning process and our New Playwrights Programme.

The Abbey produces an annual programme of diverse, engaging, innovative Irish and international theatre. We place the writer and theatre-maker at the heart of all that we do, commissioning and producing exciting new work and creating discourse and debate on the political, cultural and social issues of the day. We connect with a new generation of theatre-goers through our Engage and Learn activities and through our popular Abbey Talks series.

In 1911 the Abbey Theatre first toured internationally. With a world-class reputation, the Abbey Theatre continues to tour taking on the role of an ambassador for Irish arts and culture worldwide.

Annie Horniman provided crucial financial support to the Abbey in its first years and many others have followed her lead by investing in and supporting our work. Now more than ever, we need support to ensure we continue to fuel the flame our founders lit over a century ago.

W.B. Yeats agus an Bantiarna Augusta Gregory a bhunaigh Amharclann na Mainistreach, amharclann náisiúnta na hÉireann, i 1904, d'fhonn na smaointe agus na mothúcháin ba dhoimhne de chuid na hÉireann a láithriú ar an stáitse. Riamh anall ón uair a d'oscail sí a doirse den chéad uair, bhí, agus tá, ról ríthábhachtach agus go deimhin, ról a bhí sách conspóideach go minic, ag Amharclann na Mainistreach i saol liteartha, sóisialta agus cultúrtha na hÉireann.

In imeacht na mblianta, rinne Amharclann na Mainistreach saothar mórdhrámadóirí ar nós J.M. Synge agus Sean O'Casey a chothú agus a chéadléiriú, mar a rinne sí freisin i gcás clasaicigh chomhaimseartha ó dhrámadóirí amhail Sebastian Barry, Marina Carr, Bernard Farrell, Brian Friel, Frank McGuinness, Thomas Kilroy, Tom MacIntyre, Tom Murphy, Mark O'Rowe, Billy Roche agus Sam Shepard. Leanaimid de thacaíocht a thabhairt do nuasríbhneoireacht na hÉireann in Amharclann na Mainistreach trínár bpróiseas coimisiúnúcháin agus ár gClár do Dhrámadóirí Nua.

Léiríonn Amharclann na Mainistreach clár amharclannaíochta as Éirinn agus ó thíortha thar lear in aghaidh na bliana atá ilghnéitheach, tarraingteach agus nuálach. Cuirimid an scríbhneoir agus an t-amharclannóir i gcroílár an uile ní a dhéanaimid, agus saothar nua spreagúil á choimisiúnú agus á léiriú againn agus dioscúrsa agus díospóireacht á chruthú i dtaobh cheisteanna polaitiúla, cultúrtha agus sóisialta na linne. Cruthaímid nasc leis an nglúin nua gnáthóirí amharclainne trínar ngníomhaíochtaí 'Téigh i ngleic leis agus Foghlaim' agus tríd an tsraith cainteanna dár gcuid a bhfuil an-tóir orthu.

I 1911 is ea a chuaigh complacht Amharclann na Mainistreach ar camchuairt idirnáisiúnta den chéad uair. Anois, agus cáil dhomhanda uirthi, leanann Amharclann na Mainistreach uirthi i mbun camchuairte agus í ina hambasadóir ar fud an domhain d'ealaíona agus cultúr na hÉireann.

Sholáthair Annie Horniman tacaíocht airgid ríthábhachtach don Mhainistir siar i mblianta tosaigh na hamharclainne agus lean iliomad daoine eile an dea-shampla ceannródaíochta sin uaithi ó shin trí infheistíocht a dhéanamh inár gcuid oibre agus tacaíocht a thabhairt dúinn. Anois thar aon am eile, tá tacaíocht ag teastáil uainn lena chinntiú go leanfaimid den lóchrann sin a d'adhain ár mbunaitheoirí breis agus céad bliain ó shin a choinneáil ar lasadh.

Writer, Creative Team & Cast

NANCY HARRIS

WRITER

NANCY HARRIS IS currently the Pearson Playwright in Residence 2011 at the Bush Theatre, London. Theatre credits include *The Kreutzer Sonata* (Gate Theatre, London), *Little Dolls* (Bush Theatre Broken Space Season) and *Love in a Glass Jar* (Abbey Theatre 20 Love Season). She has also been a writer on attachment at the Soho Theatre and National Theatre Studio, London, respectively. Her radio credits include *Love in a Glass Jar* and the five part *Woman's Hour* drama series *Blood in the Bridal Shop* co-written with Louise Ramsden, both for BBC Radio 4. Nancy has also written for television.

WAYNE JORDAN

DIRECTOR

WAYNE IS AN Associate Artist of the Abbey Theatre and was the inaugural trainee director on a new mentoring programme devised by the Abbey Theatre. He directed *The Plough and the Stars, Christ Deliver Us!* (Best Director nomination, Irish Times Theatre Awards 2010), *Seven Jewish Children* and *La Dispute*. He was assistant director on *An Ideal Husband, Terminus, Kicking a Dead Horse, Julius Caesar, Alice Trilogy* and *Portia Coughlan* at the Abbey Theatre. Wayne directed *Celebration* at the Gate Theatre in the Ulster Bank Dublin Theatre Festival 2010. He is a graduate of the Samuel Beckett Centre, Trinity College Dublin. He is Artistic Director of Randolf SD | The Company and is part of Project Catalyst, an initiative of Project Arts Centre. Most of Wayne's own work has been at Project Arts Centre, where he directed *Ellamenope Jones, Everybody Loves Sylvia* (Best Director nomination Irish Times Theatre Awards 2009), *Fewer Emergencies, The Public, The Drowned World, The Illusion* and *Eeeugh!topia* for his own company and he designed *Hedwig and The Angry Inch* for Making Strange, *Stuck* for Project Arts Centre and *The Maids* for Loose Canon. Other work includes *La Voix Humaine* (Dublin Fringe Festival), *Agamemnon, Baal* (Samuel Beckett Theatre) and *Crave* (Samuel Beckett Theatre and Studiobühne, Cologne). Most recently he directed and designed *Alice in Funderland*, a work in progress musical with THISISPOPBABY at Project Arts Centre.

PAUL KEOGAN

SET & LIGHTING DESIGN

PAUL'S LIGHTING DESIGNS for the Abbey Theatre include *B for Baby, No Escape, Macbeth, Ages of the Moon, The Rivals, The Comedy of Errors, Marble, Lay Me Down Softly, The Resistible Rise of Arturo Ui, Big Love, Romeo and Juliet, Woman and Scarecrow, Julius Caesar, The School for Scandal, Homeland, The Electrocution of Children, Amazing Grace, Living Quarters, Making History, The Map Maker's Sorrow, Cúirt an Mheán Oíche, Mrs Warren's Profession, Eden, Bailegangáire, Down the Line, The Wild Duck, The Cherry Orchard, Portia Coughlan* and *Heavenly Bodies*. Other recent designs include *Boss Grady's Boys* (Gaiety Theatre), *Penelope, The Walworth Farce* (Druid), *The Crucible* (Open Air Theatre, Regent's Park, London), *Wake* (Nationale Reisopera, Netherlands), *Underneath the Lintel* (Landmark Productions), *All Over Town* (Calipo), *Plasticine, medEia, The Hairy Ape, Woyzeck* (Corcadorca), *Die Zauberflöte* (National Opera of Korea), *The Taming of the Shrew* (Royal Shakespeare Company), *Les Liaisons Dangereuses, Performances, Gates of Gold, Festen, The Deep Blue Sea, The Old Curiosity Shop* (Gate Theatre), *Tartuffe* (Playhouse Liverpool), *Intemperance* (Everyman, Liverpool), *Harvest* (Royal Court, London), *Blue / Orange* (Crucible, Sheffield), *Born Bad, In Arabia We'd All be Kings* (Hampstead, London), *The Makropulos Case, Un Ballo in Maschera, Der Fliegende Holländer* (Opera Zuid, Netherlands), *Quay West, Blasted, Far Away* (Bedrock Productions), *Chair, Angel Babel* (Operating Theatre), *Catalyst* (Rex Levitates / National Ballet of China Beijing), *The Lighthouse* (Cantiere Internazionale d'Arte, Montepulciano, Italy), *Snegurochka, The Mines of Sulphur, Susannah, Pénélope, Transformations* (Wexford Festival Opera), *Dead Man Walking, Turandot* and *Lady Macbeth of Mtensk* (Opera Ireland). Paul is an associate artist with Once Off Productions with whom he devised and directed *Man of Aran, Re-imagined*.

DONNA GERAGHTY

COSTUME DESIGN

DONNA IS A costume assistant in the Abbey Theatre Costume Department. Her previous costume design work at the Abbey Theatre includes *No Escape*. Other costume design credits include *Big Ole Piece of Cake* (Fishamble), *The Townlands of Brazil* (Axis Theatre),

End Time, Playground and Olive Skin, Blood Mouth (Gaiety School of Acting degree shows), *Red Light Winter, How To Act Around Cops and Shooters* (Purple Heart Theatre Company) and *One For Sorrow and Two For A G*irl (Skipalong Theatre Company). Donna is a graduate of the National College of Art and Design and Inchicore College of Further Education.

CARL KENNEDY
MUSIC & SOUND DESIGN

CARL'S WORK AT the Abbey Theatre includes *Only an Apple* and *The Comedy of Errors*. He was also assistant sound designer on *The Resistible Rise of Arturo Ui*. Other music and sound design work includes *Celebrity* (Peer To Peer), *Ellamenope Jones, Everybody Loves Sylvia* (Randolf SD | The Company), *Philadelphia, Here I Come!* (Gaiety Theatre), *The Girl Who Forgot to Sing Badly, The Giant Blue Hand* (The Ark / Theatre Lovett), *Little Gem, Meltdown* (Gúna Nua), *Doughnuts, Light Signals, Skin and Blister* (TEAM Theatre), *The Last Days of Judas Iscariot* (Making Strange), *Phaedra's Love* (Loose Canon), *Black Milk, Scarborough, Right Here Right Now* (Prime Cut), *All*

Over Town (Calipo), *The Infant* (Mirari Productions), *End of the Line* (Cork Midsummer Festival 2008), *Love's Labour's Lost* (Samuel Beckett Theatre), *Howie the Rookie* (Granary Theatre, Cork), *They Never Froze Walt Disney* (Theatre Makers), *A Man in Half* with composer Nico Brown (Theatre Lovett) and *The Shawl* (Bewley's Café Theatre). He was sound designer for *Macbeth* (Siren Productions) and sound co-designer with Denis Clohessy on *Unravelling the Ribbon* (Gúna Nua). Music and sound design for youth theatre includes *The Seagull* (NYT at the Peacock), *At the Black Pig's Dyke, The Crucible* (Sligo Youth Theatre), *Beatstreet (*Action Performing in the City in Konstanz, Germany), *Ideal Homes Show, Debutantes' Cabaret* (Activate Youth Theatre) and *One Last White Horse*, co-designed with Ian Kehoe (Galway Youth Theatre).

RACHEL SULLIVAN
VIDEO DESIGN

RACHEL'S PREVIOUS WORK at the Abbey Theatre was for The Waterboys' *An Appointment with Mr. Yeats*. Other work includes designing concert shows for Aslan, *The Eurovision Song Contest* (Oslo 2010), *Cheerios Childline Concert* at the O2, *Arthur's Day – Guinness, Oxegen* and *Electric Picnic*. She founded RS Visual Design which has been responsible for recent innovations in '3D building projections' including the launch of the Convention Centre Dublin and *Unwrap Dublin* at the GPO.

STEPHEN BRENNAN
JOE

STEPHEN'S MOST RECENT work at the Abbey Theatre include *The Cavalcaders, The Grown Ups, The Burial at Thebes, That Was Then, The Sanctuary Lamp, A Life, Da* and *The Wake*. He spent several years in musicals before becoming a member of the Abbey Company in 1976 for eight years, where he played more than sixty leading and supporting roles, including the title role in the Abbey's first *Hamlet*. Recent work at the Gate Theatre includes *Jane Eyre, Present Laughter* (also Spoleto Festival, Charleston, US), *A Christmas Carol, The Real Thing, Waiting for Godot* (national and worldwide tour), *Private Lives, Old Times, The Pinter Landscape* (also Lincoln Center, New York) *Pygmalion, Pride and Prejudice, Art, Tartuffe* and *Cyrano*

de Bergerac. Other theatre credits include *Blackbird* (Landmark Productions), *Phaedra, The Life of Galileo* (Rough Magic), *Hamlet* (Second Age) and *The Shaughraun* (Albery Theatre, London). Frank n' Furter in *The Rocky Horror Show,* Petruchio in *The Taming of the Shrew* and *Oedipus* at the Gaiety are among his favourite roles. Film and television credits include *The Tudors, The Clinic, The General, The Boys from Clare, A Piece of Monologue, Waiting for Godot* (Beckett on Film), *Twice Shy, El Cid, Ballykissangel, Father Ted, Bachelor's Walk* and *Eat the Peach*.

DÁIRE CASSIDY
JOHNNY

THIS IS DÁIRE'S first time working at the Abbey Theatre. His theatre credits include *Our Town* (Mill Theatre), *Coram Boy* (Mill Theatre and O'Reilly Theatre) and he was lead singing narrator in *Joseph and His Amazing Technicolour Dreamcoat* in St. Mary's College, Dublin. He has won two silver medals in his poetry section in Draoicht (Feis Mathu, 2009 and 2010) and his team won the cup for improvisation in their section (2010). He is a fluent Irish speaker.

TINA KELLEGHER

CARMEL

TINA'S WORK AT the Abbey
Theatre includes *Only an Apple,
The Plough and The Stars, Lovers at
Versailles, The Hunt For Red Willie,
The Comedy of Errors, The Trojan
Women* and *Big Maggie.* Other
theatre work includes *A Doll's
House* (Lyric Theatre, Belfast), *The
Steward of Christendom* (Royal
Court Theatre), *Streets of Dublin*
(Tivoli Theatre), *Love and a Bottle,
Our Country's Good,* (Rough
Magic), *Canaries* (Groundwork),
*The Madam McAdam Travelling
Theatre* (Field Day), *As You Like It*
(Second Age), *Little City, Trumpets
and Raspberries, The Playboy of
The Western World* and *Factory
Girls* (Druid Theatre). Film and
television credits include *Single-
Handed, The Clinic, Showbands,
Sinners, No Tears, The Snapper,
Ballykissangel, The Hanging Gale,
Murder in Eden, Happy Ever
After* and *Scarlett.* Radio work
includes *Baldi* (BBCNI), *The Price
of Reputation, Barry Lyndon* (BBC
Radio 4), *Marrying Dad* and *Old
Punks Rule* (RTÉ).

STELLA MCCUSKER

PEG

STELLA'S WORK AT the Abbey
Theatre includes *Three Sisters,
Alice Trilogy, Portia Coughlan,
Communion, Treehouses, Philadel-
phia, Here I Come!* and *The Mai.*
She has a long association with the
Lyric Theatre Players, Belfast where
she made her debut as Kate Hard-
castle in *She Stoops to Conquer.*
She also performed in *The Beauty
Queen of Leenane* (Irish Times
Theatre Award for Best Actress),
*The Glass Menagerie, A Streetcar
Named Desire, The Good Natured
Man, Pygmalion, The Memory of
Water, Desert Lullaby* and Ibsen's
Ghosts, which also played at the
National Theatre, Oslo. Other
theatre work includes *Uncle Vanya,
The House of Bernarda Alba* (Gate
Theatre), *Endgame* (Waterfront
Studio), *At the Black Pig's Dyke,
The Loves of Cass McGuire, The
Country Boy* (Druid), *Donny Boy,
The Beggar's Opera, Electra* (Man-
chester Royal Exchange), *Medea,
Our Father* (Almeida Theatre),
*Pygmies in the Ruins, Woman and
Scarecrow* (Royal Court), *Roberto
Zucco* and *Riders to the Sea* (Royal
Shakespeare Company). Film and
television credits include *Jack
Taylor, Thief in the Night, Rule*

of Thumb, Roadkill, Pure Mule, Five Minutes of Heaven, On Home Ground, The Last Furlong, Holy Cross, Whatever Love Means, MIA Mine Forever, Errors and Omissions, So You Think You've Got Troubles, Foreign Bodies, Betrayal, This is the Sea, Monkey's Blood, Dear Sarah (Jacobs Award for Best Actress), Give My Head Peace, I Fought the Law, Making the Cut and Trivia.

JANET MORAN
LAURA

JANET'S WORK AT the Abbey Theatre includes The Recruiting Officer, The Cherry Orchard, She Stoops to Conquer, Communion (Irish Times / ESB Theatre Award nomination for Best Supporting Actress), Barbaric Comedies, The Well of the Saints and The Hostage. Other theatre credits include Freefall, Everyday, Dublin by Lamplight (The Corn Exchange), Unravelling the Ribbon (Gúna Nua), Translations (Ouroborus), Submarine Man (Upstate), Metamorphosis, Platonov (Once Off), Fables, Tales and Tatlers (Pavilion Theatre), The Crock of Gold (Storytellers), King Ubu (Finewine, Galway Arts Festival) All's Well that Ends Well

and Dancing at Lughnasa (An Grianán). Janet is a contributor to The Eamon Lowe Show on Today FM. Television and film credits include The Clinic, Fair City, Minim Rest, Career Opportunities, Love is the Drug, Breakfast on Pluto, Nothing Personal, Moll Flanders, The Butcher Boy and Trivia.

CONOR MULLEN
MICHAEL

CONOR'S WORK AT the Abbey Theatre includes Closer, Macbeth, Cathleen Ní Houlihan, The Dreaming of the Bones, Purgatory, Summer, Ghosts, You Can't Take It With You and The Gentle Island. Other theatre credits include Lady Windemere's Fan (Gate Theatre), After the Gods (Hampstead Theatre), Carthaginians (Druid), Equus, Observe the Sons of Ulster Marching Towards the Somme (Red Kettle), Torchlight and Laserbeams and Borstal Boy (Gaiety Theatre). Recent television credits include Raw, Single-Handed, Anner House, Proof, When Harvey Met Bob, Rough Diamond, The Silence, Holby City, Silent Witness, Hearbeat, Murder Prevention, School Run, Island at War, Ultimate Force,

The Bill, Soldier Soldier and *The Whistleblowers*. Films include *The Honeymooners, Puckoon, Saltwater, Ordinary Decent Criminal, Silent Grace, The Tiger's Tail* and *Three Wise Women*.

NATALIE RADMALL-QUIRKE

GAIL

NATALIE'S WORK AT the Abbey Theatre includes *The Plough and the Stars, The Comedy of Errors* and *An Ideal Husband*. She is a founding member of Randolf SD | The Company. Theatre credits include *Ellamenope Jones, Everybody Loves Sylvia, The Illusion, Eeeugh!topia* (Randolf SD | The Company, Project Arts Centre), *Celebration, Jane Eyre* (Gate Theatre), *The Birthday of the Infanta* (Bewley's Café Theatre), *Moment* (Tall Tales), *Mud* (Gate Theatre, London), *I Witness* (Finborough Theatre), *Footfalls* (Players Theatre) and *Crave* (Samuel Beckett Centre and Studiobühne, Cologne). Radio work includes *In Praise of Darkness, A Proper Da* and *Comfort and Joy*. Natalie trained at Trinity College Dublin and LAMDA.

If you
VALUE THEATRE
you'll love these great opportunities...

Abbey Member

BECOMING A MEMBER of the Abbey Theatre puts you at the top of the queue by giving you great discounts and free access to talks. Sign up today and enjoy Member Benefits that include:

- Half-price tickets for Abbey stage previews
- Up to €5 off tickets for Abbey Theatre productions
- Priority booking period
- Free access to the Abbey Talks

Member €25

Joint Member €40
(for two people)

...

Benefits subject to availability. For terms and conditions see www.abbeytheatre.ie.

Abbey Friend

AS A FRIEND you can enjoy all the benefits of being a Member, plus behind the scenes insight and a closer association with the Abbey Theatre. Friend Benefits also include:

- Two tickets to a production of your choice
- Invitations to Friends' nights
- Opportunity to buy tickets for Opening Night performances
- Programme listing

Friend €125

Joint Friend €230
(for two people)

...

Joint Friends get four tickets instead of two and double the invitations.

TO JOIN pick up a form from the Abbey Foyer, join online at www.abbeytheatre.ie or call (01) 879 7244. If you are interested in supporting the Abbey Theatre as a **Patron** (€500) or **Platinum Patron** (€1000) please email development@abbeytheatre.ie or call us on (01) 887 2223 for more details.

Next at the Abbey Theatre ...

TWO WORLD PREMIERES

11 MARCH – 16 APRIL / 18 MARCH - 16 APRIL

THE PASSING / THE EAST PIER

Written and directed by

Paul Mercier

---

12 – 30 APRIL

The Ark in association with Theatre Lovett

THE GIRL WHO FORGOT TO SING BADLY

Finegan Kruckemeyer

---

27 APRIL – 11 JUNE

PYGMALION

Bernard Shaw

WORLD PREMIERE | 25 MAY – 25 JUNE

PERVE

Stacey Gregg

---

23 JUNE – 13 AUGUST

TRANSLATIONS

Brian Friel

*For booking information visit **www.abbeytheatre.ie** or call **(01) 87 87 222***

NO ROMANCE

Nancy Harris

For my mother and father

Note on the Text

[ ] indicates a word or sentence that is not spoken, but conveyed in the playing

… indicates an unfinished or unarticulated thought

– indicates a very brief pause or a beat where a thought is being clarified

 / indicates the point at which the next speaker interrupts

Time

Ireland, present day.

Sets should be spare and not necessarily naturalistic. Props are referred to in the text but how much detail and furniture is needed is entirely up to the vision of the director and designer.

The main concern is that each story is able to move fluidly into the next.

This text went to press before the end of rehearsals and so may differ slightly from the play as performed.

Author's Note

I would like to thank Fiach Mac Conghail and Aideen Howard at the Abbey Theatre for commissioning and supporting *No Romance* since its inception.

I would also like to express my heartfelt gratitude and appreciation to the following – Wayne Jordan, Rochelle Stevens, Julia Molony, Holly Ni Chiardha, Claire Everett, Mary Devally, Anthony Weigh, Roisin McBrinn, Heather Thornton, Jimmy Fay, The Irish Cancer Society and The Peggy Ramsey Foundation.

And lastly my family – Anne, Eoghan, Connie, Mungo and MirKev. For everything.

4

Characters

ONE

LAURA, *thirty-six – a client wanting to be photographed. When she talks, she talks.*

GAIL, *thirty-six – the photographer. Restrained, but not unkind.*

TWO

CARMEL, *late forties – works in a bank. Nicely dressed for the occasion.*

JOE, *fifties – currently not working. Carmel's husband.*

THREE

PEG, *eighty.*

MICHAEL, *forty-two – her son. A hard-working, harassed aura.*

JOHNNY, *twelve – Peg's grandson, Michael's son. Quiet, awkward. Holds a Sony PSP.*

ONE

The living room of an upmarket apartment in Dublin's city centre, now being used as a makeshift photographic studio.

The room is sparse and white and with very little furniture in it except for lights, a camera and a stool. There may also be a small makeshift screen for changing behind somewhere in a corner. A bag of 'costumes' LAURA has brought for the shoot sits on the floor.

A large white muslin sheet hangs against the walls. On the far wall, the muslin sheet hides an open space – like a window in the wall – that looks out into the hall. It is one of those architectural quirks of an expensive modern apartment that serves no real purpose other than to make the room a bit different. In this instance, because of the bright lights and the muslin cloth, anyone passing in the hall is lit up in silhouette.

LAURA *stands in the middle of the room, heavily made-up and wearing what looks like a makeshift medieval costume with a slightly sexy twist. She looks vaguely ridiculous.*

The two women stare at one another for a beat.

GAIL. Okay.

LAURA. Sorry.

GAIL. No /

LAURA. It's a bit of a shock, I can tell by your face.

GAIL. It's – no, it's not a shock, it's just /

LAURA. Not what you were expecting.

GAIL. Well /

LAURA. It's alright. It was my sister's bridesmaid dress. It's a bit small for me – she's a ten. I'm a fourteen. On a good week. And actually it doesn't go up all the way at the back. See?

GAIL. Oh /

LAURA. But I thought, you know, that that might be good because it might look a bit – you know.

GAIL. Yes.

LAURA. Because I want it to be tight.

GAIL. Sure.

LAURA. I want it to be vampish.

GAIL. Yes.

LAURA. That's sort of the point.

GAIL. Of course.

LAURA. And I have a wand too.

GAIL. A wand?

>   LAURA *rummages in the bag of clothes. Pulls out a wand.*

LAURA. Ta-da.

GAIL. Oh – yes, you meant a – wand-wand. I see.

>   LAURA *holds up the wand.*

>   So you're a – fairy?

LAURA. Well, no. More like a princess-type thing. I think.

GAIL. Right.

LAURA. That was the idea.

GAIL. It's just – I thought it you said you were going for a medieval look.

LAURA. Well, yeah, I am. It is medieval. A medieval princess.

GAIL. I see.

LAURA. I was thinking Guinevere. Though she was a Queen, but maybe a Queen's more – I mean, as long as it's not a drag queen. I don't look like a drag queen, do I?

GAIL. No /

LAURA. It's Knights of the Round Table I'm going for but I don't want to be mistaken for the knight /

GAIL. No /

LAURA. If you get me. Cos they were all pretty saucy, weren't they? Those knights in their gear. They were always off having affairs and whatnot. With comely maidens and other people's wives. I mean, look at Guinevere.

GAIL *nods*.

GAIL. Hmmn.

Then confesses.

I actually don't know anything about – Guinevere.

LAURA. Oh, she was fabulous, Guinevere. She was King Arthur's wife, which was – quite a coup at the time. She was a Queen so technically she had it all, but she was unhappy because Arthur was off being King and spending all his time with his armies or what have you and she's alone with a sewing kit. Then one day she meets Arthur's handsome knight, Lancelot, who awakens her passions and is sensitive to her needs – one imagines. They fall madly in love and have a big torrid affair, which Arthur finds out about, and he sentences Guinevere to death. On a fire.

GAIL. Fire?

LAURA. Or a pyre.

GAIL. God.

LAURA. Yeah. But Lancelot rescues her and takes her away. And there's a war of course – there usually is – and then she goes off and has to join a nunnery and… well, that's the end of that.

GAIL. Right.

LAURA. It's always the fucking nunnery in the end.

GAIL. I had no idea you were such an – expert on all this.

LAURA. Oh, I love all those old love stories. I love love stories. I'm going on, aren't I? You have to stop me.

GAIL. No. It's good to – have a context for [all this]… So you're – Guinevere then?

LAURA. Well, I suppose. That was sort of – I mean – I didn't really – I didn't exactly pin anything down – in my head. But that was sort of my idea with the dress and stuff… Guinevere. What do you think?

LAURA *stands up straight and holds out the wand.* GAIL *surveys her.*

GAIL. I think the wand is a bit confusing.

LAURA. Really?

GAIL. It's a bit – Disney.

LAURA. Oh.

GAIL. I don't understand what a medieval queen is doing with a wand. Wands aren't real – if she were there with a goblet or something, I'd believe it, but a wand…

LAURA *looks at the wand somewhat disheartened.*

I think if you're going to be medieval, be medieval, you know.

LAURA. You're right. God – wand. I don't know what I was thinking. Of course she wouldn't have a wand. No one has a wand.

GAIL. No.

LAURA. I think I just liked the idea of holding something.

LAURA *puts the wand down.*

Would a riding crop be better?

GAIL. I think you're fine as you… are.

Beat.

LAURA. Are you sure you're alright with all this?

GAIL. Me?

LAURA. Cos I know it's a bit /

GAIL. I'm fine /

LAURA. Not your usual run-of-the-mill Monday morning. Probably.

GAIL. There are no usual Monday mornings.

LAURA. That's what I sort of thought. When I saw your website and the sort of stuff you're doing now with the transsexuals and the girls in the red-light district and the – lady boys, I thought – Gail's the one, Gail's the one I should go to for this, she'll get it. And now I find you're writing a book.

GAIL. Well, no /

LAURA. I always knew you'd be famous.

GAIL. Not writing.

LAURA. Publishing.

GAIL. Hoping to publish.

LAURA. Your very own book.

GAIL. Yes.

LAURA. With your very own words.

GAIL. Yes. Well, no. There's no real words. Or if there are, someone else will – I might write the foreword but mainly – mainly it's a collection of my photographs. Over the years.

LAURA. That's bloody brilliant, isn't it?

GAIL. Yes. Well, it will be. If it goes ahead. If this meeting today goes well. But I mean – there are no guarantees – so let's not get ahead of ourselves.

GAIL *starts to set up the room.*

LAURA. Did you always know you were going to be famous?

GAIL. What?

LAURA. In school? Did you always know deep down you'd be better than everyone else?

GAIL. No.

LAURA. Ah you did.

GAIL. Don't be silly.

LAURA. Course you did.

GAIL. I did not.

LAURA. You had an aura. Everyone used say.

GAIL. No they didn't.

LAURA. They did so. It was because you never used to speak. And you were great at art.

GAIL. Art?

LAURA. Remember you won a hundred pounds for that collage of an owl you did?

GAIL. What owl?

LAURA. Big huge thing, it was. With mad eyes and real feathers. They hung it up in assembly hall. Do you not remember?

GAIL. I – vaguely /

LAURA. Oh, it was fantastic. And we were all green when you got the cheque because a hundred pounds at the time was like –

GAIL (*remembering*). God, yes. You're – I did win something /

LAURA. I mean, you deserved it. The hundred quid – no question about that. No one else thought of putting real feathers on their owls. That was a stroke of proper genius.

GAIL. And here, I've always thought the only thing I got out of school was a thick skin.

LAURA. Oh. Yeah. There were some real bitches in our year, weren't there?

GAIL. Yes, there were.

LAURA. They gave you a pretty hard time, didn't they?

GAIL. Yes they did.

LAURA. But where are they now, eh? Not off travelling the world. Not off taking pictures and meeting eunuchs and publishing books of their photographs.

GAIL. Well, I don't travel so much these days.

The two women look at one another.

LAURA. I'm sorry I'm so early.

GAIL. Early?

LAURA. This morning. It's just – I work nights now so –

GAIL. No, early's good for me. Especially with this meeting. Good to have a distraction.

LAURA. Would have been nice to have had a glass of wine or something though. To loosen me up a bit before I – unleash my inner… whatever. Diva.

GAIL. Would you like a glass of wine?

LAURA. No, no. I was only saying /

GAIL. Cos we probably have some somewhere.

LAURA. Ah no. Wouldn't think that's a good idea. Not at nine o'clock in the morning. Sure if I start now – I mightn't be able to stop.

LAURA laughs, maybe a bit too loudly, then stops.

GAIL. Well, just let me know. It's important that you feel at ease.

LAURA. Is it?

GAIL. So we get the best picture.

On the muslin cloth we see the shadow of a woman walk by in the hallway.

LAURA. Right. (*Pointing at the cloth.*) Would you look at that. Like shadow puppets.

GAIL. Oh – yes. Sorry. She won't do that again.

LAURA suddenly becomes self-conscious.

LAURA. She can't see me, can she?

GAIL. No, no – you're perfectly safe. It's just – it can mess up the lighting.

LAURA. Oh.

Perhaps GAIL *starts to set up the camera.*

GAIL. This place isn't really an ideal studio.

LAURA. Is it not, no?

GAIL. My old studio was in town but – rents.

LAURA. Well, here is great. I'm happy here. I love having a nose around other people's houses. It's so – white.

GAIL. Like a hospital.

LAURA.…A nice one.

GAIL. Don't know what possessed us buying this place.

LAURA. Ah no. This is gorgeous. I'd kill to live somewhere like this – you're near the sea, you can walk into town.

GAIL. I can sit in my living room and look into the hallway as people pass by.

LAURA. Sorry?

GAIL. That hole in the wall behind the cloth literally serves no purpose. I mean, I assume it's meant to be some sort of – window, but why they put it there… Architectural masturbation.

LAURA. Maybe it's for decoration.

GAIL. A window that looks onto the sea has a point. A window that looks into the hall, is a hole.

LAURA. You could – fill it up. If you wanted.

GAIL. Sarah likes it. She thinks it's airy. She hates that I've put those over it but what are you going to do. Do you want to stand here, so I can test the light?

LAURA *walks over and steps in front of the camera.*

LAURA. Oh. Sure.

GAIL *looks at* LAURA *through the lens.* LAURA *tries to act nonchalant.*

She's very tolerant then. Sarah. Letting you work at home like this.

GAIL. Hmmmn.

LAURA. I mean – where's all your furniture?

GAIL. Bedrooms. Look up for a second.

GAIL takes a picture, testing the light.

LAURA. Two-bed, is it?

GAIL. Yes. Again.

GAIL takes another.

LAURA. We only have one. Bedroom. I'd love a place of our own but Simon says – Simon says – that's our little thing.

GAIL smiles.

Worn off a bit now but it was good at the start.

GAIL. Isn't it always.

LAURA. Yeah. (*Getting it.*) Yeah. Well, Simon says renting's the future and we should keep renting even after we're married cos that's what they do in Switzerland and he's a big fan of the Swiss – should I be doing something with my hands?

GAIL. Just relax.

LAURA. Okay.

Whatever LAURA does she doesn't look that relaxed. GAIL takes one more picture, then stands up – suddenly all business.

GAIL. So. How do we want to do this?

LAURA. Do what?

GAIL. Guinevere.

LAURA. Oh. Oh, well, I don't know. I mean… what do you think?

GAIL. I – well, I thought you had something in mind.

LAURA. Right.

GAIL. On the phone you said you had some ideas.

LAURA. Well, I did – yeah – I did have one or two – rough ideas in my head, but now you know, now that we're here – in your – studio I'm wondering if they were a bit…

GAIL. What?

LAURA. Unrealistic.

GAIL. Well, what were they?

LAURA. Well, no because – I mean it was – I wasn't really – with the wand and everything. I wasn't really thinking straight was I?

GAIL. Well, what *were* you thinking about – roughly?

LAURA. It's stupid.

GAIL. What was your starting point?

LAURA. Starting point?

GAIL. How did you even come up with this idea in the first place?

LAURA. …It's going to sound a bit strange.

GAIL. I've photographed hermaphrodites, Laura.

    LAURA *takes a deep breath*.

LAURA. I read a blog. Online. The Story of 'C'. Do you know it?

GAIL. The Story of – C?

LAURA. It has quite a following.

GAIL. I've always thought people who write blogs should be medicated.

LAURA. Oh me too, me too. [Total nut jobs.] 'Get a bit of sun, why don't you.' Normally I wouldn't have much time for them. Only this girl in work got me onto it. She's hooked. On the blog. Said I had to check it out. So I did.

GAIL. The Story of C.

LAURA. Yes.

GAIL. What does the 'C' stand for?

LAURA. I'm not sure. I mean, it could be her initial. The woman who writes it, because she doesn't use her real name.

GAIL. No.

LAURA. Because of the subject matter.

GAIL. Yes.

LAURA.…Sex.

GAIL. I gathered.

LAURA. Well, it's erotica. But like it's sort of – tasteful erotica. Well, it's not tasteful, but it's not complete pornography. It's more like – stories or what have you – with a… twist. And every week she posts up a different one.

GAIL. C?

LAURA. Exactly. She writes about different characters having sort of sexy adventures. Sometimes they're ordinary people that she's just made up out of her head, but sometimes – they're ones out of history or mythology like Dido or Guinevere or Queen Medb of Connaught. You know?

It's clear that GAIL *doesn't.*

From the epic pre-Christian Irish story, *The Táin Bó Cúailnge*?

GAIL. I need to brush up on my pre-Christian era.

LAURA. Oh. Medb was another one. A warrior queen. Fearless with her sexuality. Whole armies between her thighs she had apparently – and not a bother on her. Used to make the men stop battle when she had her period and everything.

GAIL. Wow.

LAURA. I know. See, that's what I like about this C woman. Not only is she good on the erotic stuff but very often you get to learn a bit too.

GAIL. Educational then.

LAURA. And a lot of her stories are set in Ireland which I like, because you can really visualise the location. Glendalough, Newgrange – you wanna see what she has going on on top of the Hill of Tara – very inventive.

GAIL. I can imagine /

LAURA. So anyway, I read this blog and I got this idea to do a series of pictures. Sort of based on it. Loosely. I mean, the blog doesn't have any pictures, she just writes stories, but I thought – I thought I could dress up as some of the characters from her stories. Sort of use them as inspiration. I thought that would make a great present because. Well, because Simon likes it when I dress up.

GAIL. Okay. Well /

LAURA *is getting into it now.*

LAURA. Like I was thinking it would be great to get a picture of me as Guinevere sitting up on a big white horse.

GAIL. A horse?

LAURA. Or what have you. And maybe showing a bit of leg – or whatever.

GAIL. A – horse?

LAURA. Or something. Something really different. I mean, I don't want them to look cheap, I want them to look classy. Do you remember that book *Sex* that Madonna brought out years ago?

GAIL. But – where would we get a horse?

LAURA. Well, I don't know – the horse was just an idea. Obviously you don't have a horse here and I suppose it was easy for Madonna given her level of income. We're constrained by budgets and time and –

GAIL. Location.

LAURA. Yeah.

GAIL. Not too many white horses around Pearse Street these days.

LAURA. No. But you know what I mean… maybe we could Photoshop in a horse?

GAIL. I'm not sure that'll look very good.

LAURA. No. No, maybe not.

LAURA *is suddenly self-conscious.*

I realise – I realise – saying this that it probably sounds a bit… I was just throwing out some ideas because you were asking about my starting point. And that… well, that was my starting point.

GAIL. And it's a great starting point. It's a very – imaginative starting point. But I think if this is going to work – we're going to have to – refine our expectations – somewhat. Work with what we have here. You know?

LAURA *looks around the room.*

LAURA. Sure. Okay.

GAIL. In my experience less is always more for a good picture.

The silhouette of a woman walking past carrying two cups of coffee can be seen on the wall.

What *is* she doing?

LAURA. I don't mind.

GAIL. No but – we have a deal. When I'm here with a client, no one goes to the kitchen. I could have been in the middle of a shot there. That shadow could have been thrown right across your face. If she does it again, I swear –

LAURA *smiles.*

LAURA. It's mad how easily we lose the rag with the people we love, isn't it? I get so annoyed with Simon sometimes, I could stab him in the eye with a plastic fork and watch him bleed to death on the floor. Then five seconds later – it's gone and I can't remember what I was annoyed about in the first place.

GAIL. It's different. She knows.

GAIL *starts to assess* LAURA *again. Maybe walks around her.*

LAURA. Does – Sarah not work?

GAIL. She does.

LAURA. At home?

GAIL. She's a doctor.

LAURA. Oh. A doctor. Shouldn't she be off – fixing people then?

GAIL. You would think.

GAIL *points to* LAURA*'s outfit.*

You know, I'm wondering if Guinevere is really the right one for us to start off with here.

LAURA *looks down at herself.*

LAURA. I could tell you didn't like it.

GAIL. It isn't that I don't – like it.

LAURA. It's okay. Honesty is good. Honesty's what I'm here for. If there was one person I knew wouldn't blow smoke up my arse it was you, Gail.

GAIL. Well, that's – very flattering but I just – wonder if Guinevere is a bit – full-on, you know. For a first shot. We might be better off with something a little more – understated, you know. To begin with. Maybe you could talk me through some of your other – suggestions.

LAURA *looks at* GAIL *quizzically.* GAIL *points to the bag of clothes.*

From your bag there.

LAURA. Right, okay. Yes. My – suggestions. Alright – I mean, they're just – they're not – I'm not sure what I put in here now to be honest.

GAIL. Well, let's just have a look at what there is.

LAURA. Okay. Yeah. Let's see.

LAURA *goes to the bag and starts rummaging around, pulling out bits and pieces. It's awkward. She tries for small talk.*

So, em, you and – Sarah – have been together a long time, have you?

GAIL. You could say that, yes.

LAURA. That's lovely.

She pulls out something – shows it to GAIL.

I thought this was a bit Cleopatra-esque. You know?

GAIL. Oh – right.

She discards it quickly, carries on.

LAURA. But maybe not. How long's long?

GAIL. About ten years.

LAURA. Ten years?

GAIL. Something like that.

LAURA. Jesus, that's *really* long.

GAIL. Hmmnn.

LAURA. That's an entire decade.

GAIL. Yes.

LAURA. God. A decade. I could be dead in a decade.

GAIL. Well, we all could, I suppose.

LAURA. Yeah, I suppose.

GAIL. But let's hope not.

LAURA. No, but that's great. That's really… You must be real soulmates.

GAIL. Well, what's soulmates when you get down to it?

LAURA *looks at her in admiration.*

LAURA. And I remember when you told everyone you were a lesbian.

GAIL. Oh God.

LAURA. The night of the debs. Jaws literally hit the ground all around the dance floor. 'Posh Gail's a lesbian.' I'll never forget it.

GAIL. Me neither.

LAURA. I thought it was so chic.

GAIL. It was like being an exhibit at a science fair.

LAURA. Ah no /

GAIL. First real-life lesbian most people had ever laid eyes on. You could see the curtains twitching for weeks afterwards.

LAURA. God – yeah. I never – I just thought you were great. For being yourself. But obviously – obviously it must have been hard.

GAIL *shudders*.

GAIL. I wouldn't go back if you paid me.

LAURA. But ten years is… Ten months is a long relationship for me. Was. Before I met Simon. Ten minutes. Well, not ten minutes but you know what I – I'd terrible luck with men. Terrible taste. A fella could've been sucking on a bottle of vodka while robbing the purse from my handbag and I'd convince myself he was the man of my dreams.

GAIL. Oh now /

LAURA. You want to have seen some of the chancers I went out with. Should've had my head examined.

GAIL. We've all made bad choices I'm sure.

LAURA *pulls out a red lacy bodice and feather boa, delighted*.

LAURA. Here. What about this?

GAIL. Oh. That's – yeah – interesting.

LAURA. Sort of a Moulin Rouge type of thing.

GAIL. Hmmmn.

She pulls out a top hat.

LAURA. With this. And some hot pants or something.

GAIL. Yes. Okay. I mean, it's still a bit /

LAURA. Simon bought me this corset. Picked it out himself and everything, bless him. If you knew Simon, he's really not the Ann Summers type. Probably took him a week to recover. It's kind of a pain with all the laces and stuff but – if I could pull it off, he'd be in his element I reckon. He loves the whole chorus-girl can-can thing. I could put on some stockings too – for the whole shebang. What do you think?

LAURA pulls out some gloves. GAIL *clocks her expectant expression.*

GAIL. Sure, give it a go. Maybe I can do something with the light. Silhouette you a bit.

LAURA. Ooh.

GAIL. Or something.

LAURA. Great.

The figure passes again in the hallway – the shadow on the muslin cloth.

GAIL. Jesus. (*Calling.*) Sarah!

LAURA smiles and gathers up the clothes.

LAURA. I'll only be a sec.

LAURA goes behind the changing screen. The figure goes past in the hall again, maybe this time towel-drying her hair. GAIL *is about to call her name, doesn't.*

(*From behind the screen.*) So tell us how do you do it?

GAIL. What?

LAURA. Keep the romance going over ten years? You must have some tips.

GAIL. Oh. I don't know. You – probably have a better idea of all that than I do. You're the one making a sexy photo album. What do you think the 'C' really stands for?

GAIL *starts to go through the bag of clothes that* LAURA
*has brought, drawing out different eclectic items. A French
maid's outfit, a duster, handcuffs, etc.*

LAURA. I don't know.

GAIL. Clitoris?

LAURA. That's a bit vulgar.

GAIL. It's a sex blog. What about –

LAURA. Don't say it.

GAIL. What?

LAURA *peers around the screen.*

LAURA. That. What you were going to – I don't like it.

GAIL. Which?

LAURA. Cunt. I know we're s'posed to reclaim it as women
and it's all over the television and what have you these days,
but it's just not my cup of – I think it sounds vicious. It
sounds like something that'd cut you. And I don't think it's
what the 'C' stands for anyway because the stories she writes
are much more poetic.

GAIL (*disbelieving*). Poetic.

LAURA. She has a little routine, this C woman. She goes
through it before she writes each story. Every week, the
same. She says she puts on some music, pours herself a
drink, closes her eyes and calls in her muses.

GAIL. Calls in her muses?

LAURA. I know it sounds –

GAIL. Her sex muses?

LAURA. But I think it's a good little touch – I like the ritual of
it. Even Simon agrees there's something nice about it.

GAIL. You read Simon the blog?

LAURA. Just for a laugh. You should read some to Sarah some
time. Spice things up a bit. Not that you – need to or
anything but… if you want.

GAIL *looks down.*

LAURA *goes back behind the changing screen.*

GAIL *starts to go through the bag again.*

GAIL. So you've been with Simon how long?

LAURA. A year. Almost to the day now. One of those whirlwind jobs. I asked him out – if you can believe that. He arrived at the club this time last year to celebrate his birthday. And he had such a face on him the whole night because he doesn't like loud music and he doesn't like his birthday. And I was bringing them drinks and making jokes and eventually I got so sick of looking at him I said, 'Here, Mister Sourpuss, if you give me a smile, I'll buy you dinner on my night off.' And he did.

GAIL. That's sweet.

GAIL *pulls a pair of goggles and some flippers from the bag.*

LAURA. Well, I'd have preferred it if he'd asked me but… I'd have been waiting for ever that way. I'd probably have ended up one of those little old ladies who live all on their own and talk to themselves. Poor things.

GAIL. I doubt that.

LAURA. It's his fortieth on Saturday which is why I'm doing this. You have to do something special for a man's fortieth, don't you?

GAIL *looks in the bag. There doesn't seem to be more to this ensemble.*

GAIL. Do you?

LAURA. Yeah. Cos forty is when they start to feel old and when they feel old they get cranky. I mean, I'm not exactly a spring chicken /

GAIL *pulls out a red evening dress. It's the most sophisticated thing in the bag. Perhaps she hangs it up somewhere.*

– but I thought it was strange when I met him, you know.

That he wasn't married. I kept thinking what's wrong with him? He has a good job, he wears decent shoes, he has clean fingernails and he's not married. But then I thought – well, I'm not married. And there's nothing wrong with me. Why does everyone have to be married in this day and age?

GAIL. Not everyone *can* be married in this day and age.

LAURA *steps out from behind the screen.*

LAURA. No. Fair point.

GAIL. I was just saying /

LAURA. No, you're right. Though things are changing now, I suppose. Civil partnership.

GAIL. Well, yes.

LAURA. Now we're in the twenty-first century. Not exactly fast but… sure, can you imagine the day they face up to the fact that women in this country have abortions. Ryanair'll lose a ton of business what? Would you mind doing these laces for me? Never can manage them myself.

GAIL *starts to do up* LAURA*'s corset.*

Is this the sort of thing the girls in the red-light district wear?

GAIL. The girls in the red-light district wear a lot less.

LAURA. You can't see their faces in your pictures.

GAIL. You're not allowed to show their faces. You're not actually allowed to take pictures in the red-light district.

LAURA. God.

GAIL. 'To sell your body.' Terrifying turn of phrase when you think about it.

GAIL *ties.*

LAURA. You've seen it all, haven't you?

GAIL. Hardly.

LAURA. I never even did the year in Australia.

GAIL *ties*.

Simon thinks my job is a form of prostitution.

GAIL. You're a manageress.

LAURA. Well, hostess. That's the official [title] – He wants me to give up after we're married. Says he can't stand the thought of his wife out at night schmoozing with a bunch of drunks. But that's not exactly an accurate description of what I do. Looking after food and wine and greeting regulars.

Beat.

And I like it. That's the other thing. I'm good at it. And these days I'm lucky to have it.

A moment of silence. GAIL *ties*.

Some people think I'm mad doing this. Dirty pictures for my boyfriend. They think it's bonkers. Dressing up. Or pathetic maybe. Maybe they think it's pathetic. I don't know.

GAIL. It's none of their business what it is. Too tight?

LAURA. No. I know it isn't.

GAIL *pulls the laces in again*.

And I wouldn't be going around telling everyone either, because it's private – it's a private thing, this, it's between me and Simon… But I told my sister. The one who gave me her bridesmaid dress. Stupid. But I was excited. At first she thought it was a joke, but then she got this look on her face, like – like it was – a bit of a sad thing to be doing. For a man. And that I was somehow being a bit – desperate. Or something.

GAIL *finishes tying* LAURA*'s corset*.

GAIL. How's that?

LAURA *takes a deep breath in the corset*.

LAURA. Grand – yeah – it's…

Beat.

What do you think?

GAIL (*thinking she means the outfit*). Um… well /

    LAURA *looks at* GAIL *in the eyes.*

LAURA. Do you think it's desperate? To be doing this – for a man?

GAIL. No.

LAURA. Really?

GAIL. No. I think – I think it's very – thoughtful. It's a bit unusual…

    LAURA *suddenly starts to cry – childlike and shocking even to herself.*

    GAIL *stands and watches. Horrified.*

Oh my… Laura?

Silence. Crying.

God, Laura. I…

    GAIL *takes a step towards* LAURA.

I really didn't – have I – was that the wrong thing to…

    LAURA *keeps crying.* GAIL *takes another step towards her.*

I think it's great – what you're – all the trouble you've… and the – blog. I don't think it's desperate at all, I think it's really… creative. If more people put as much effort into their partner's birthdays – God, the world would be a far – better – oh Jesus – Laura, are you alright?

    LAURA *shakes her head. Wipes her face with her wrist.*

LAURA. I'm sorry.

GAIL. No, I'm – sorry.

LAURA. No, I'm sorry – I'm really. I'm really. I'm – I'm… Just give me a minute.

    LAURA *tries to gather herself.*

GAIL. Do you want – a tissue? Here, here have a –

GAIL *hands her a tissue*.

LAURA. I'm sorry. I can't believe this. I can't believe I'm standing here – crying. In a corset. That's just – you must think I'm for the birds.

GAIL. No. I just forget how vulnerable people feel getting their picture /

LAURA. It's not your fault.

GAIL. It's because I do this all the time and – to be honest with you, Laura, I've been a bit distracted this morning.

LAURA. Please – don't /

GAIL. Things have been sort of tense here. With Sarah.

LAURA. It isn't you. It's because I felt it.

GAIL. Hmmnn?

LAURA. I don't normally feel anything – there, but it's because it's so tight.

GAIL. You mean the corset?

LAURA. Everything's pressing and I can / feel it.

GAIL. Well, here, you should have said –

GAIL *moves to loosen it*. LAURA *stops her.*

LAURA. No. Don't.

GAIL. But I've obviously /

LAURA *tries to gather herself.*

LAURA. It's gotten bigger, you see. I mean, it feels bigger than I thought it was. The doctor said it was about the size of a large grape, but I feel like I'm carrying a small lemon. Which is actually – quite big if you think about it.

LAURA *feels around her bust.*

GAIL. I'm not sure I'm… following.

LAURA. No, course you're not. Sorry. I'm not making any… I thought I was doing really well with this whole cancer business. I thought I was really managing and not being hysterical, but it turns out – well, I guess it turns out I'm just as much of a basket case as anyone else.

GAIL. Cancer?

LAURA. Yeah.

GAIL. You – have…

LAURA. I do. Yeah. That's right. The big C. Only we know for definite what this one stands for.

She points to her breast.

GAIL. Oh my God.

LAURA. Mad, isn't it?

GAIL. But how did you – I mean when did you – I mean… why didn't you say anything?

LAURA. What do you mean?

GAIL. Why didn't you tell me?

LAURA. I am telling you.

GAIL. But I could've – I would've…

GAIL is at a loss.

Jesus, Laura, I'm really sorry.

LAURA. No, listen. Don't. Because it sounds worse than it – and I don't usually cry – I mean, that was a total – even when the tests came back and the doctor told me – I didn't cry. Because it's going to be grand. I mean, it's not going to be – grand-grand because I'm young – which isn't great. Thirty-six isn't a great age to get cancer – it tends to be aggressive.

Beat.

But they think they got it – in time and – as long as they treat it and it doesn't – you know – or come back somewhere else it's –

GAIL. Positive.

LAURA. Yeah, it's positive. That's what they keep saying.

LAURA *puts her hand up to her breast again.*

GAIL. Well, that's – good.

LAURA. Yeah. It is – good.

They look at each other.

GAIL. You don't look sick.

LAURA. I should dress like a hooker more often.

GAIL. Here, let me get you a blanket or – you must be /

GAIL *picks up whatever's nearby.*

LAURA. No I'm…

LAURA *looks at herself.*

Well, I *am* a bit cold actually now you mention it.

GAIL. Here.

LAURA. My mother got cancer.

GAIL. I know, yeah. I… remember

LAURA. Different times though. Now.

GAIL. Yes.

LAURA. So they keep saying.

GAIL *puts something round* LAURA*'s shoulders. Maybe rubs her back.*

Thanks. That's… I'm glad you're doing so well, Gail.

GAIL. Oh now.

LAURA. I know you didn't like me much in school.

GAIL. What?

LAURA. I'm glad we kept in touch though. It's funny the people you stay in touch with. You're always so busy – sometimes I feel like a stalker. I'm not, am I?

GAIL. Of course you're not.

LAURA. I mean, I know you need the business –

GAIL. I did like you in school, Laura.

LAURA. You thought I was weak.

GAIL. No I /

LAURA. It's okay. I *was* weak. In school. I wanted to be liked. You didn't care about being liked.

GAIL. That's completely /

LAURA. It's what makes you so brilliant.

> GAIL *doesn't know what to say.* LAURA *looks down.*

> They reckon lumpectomy.

GAIL. Lumpectomy?

LAURA. As treatment.

GAIL. Oh.

LAURA. Followed by chemotherapy. Then radiotherapy. Then five years on Tamoxifen.

> GAIL *looks at her, not knowing.*

> It's a drug. Stops you producing oestrogen.

GAIL. Right.

LAURA. They have it all worked out. Actually, it's not the worst as cancer operations go.

GAIL. Is it not, no?

> LAURA *looks down at her breast.*

LAURA. I *can* just have the whole thing off. That's an option too – but the doctors don't think I need to. They try to preserve as much of the tissue as possible these days. Which I suppose is a good thing. My mam lost her boob and we know how that turned out, so… I might as well hang onto mine.

GAIL. Of course.

LAURA. I'm not mad on the idea of chemo. It makes you sick and you lose your hair and – it can send you into early menopause. Do you want kids?

GAIL. Yes.

LAURA. I wanted kids. Simon [wanted kids]… I'll be forty-one when this is over. Imagine.

GAIL. Laura, look –

LAURA *pulls the blanket round herself.*

LAURA. I haven't told him yet.

GAIL. Who?

LAURA. Simon.

GAIL. Oh… Don't you think you – should?

LAURA *shrugs.*

LAURA. Can't believe I've managed it, in a way. I'm so friggin' bad at keeping secrets. Normally I'm such a bloody – yabber. To be able to lie in bed next to a man and have him snuggling up to you and kissing you and putting his hand on the very thing you know has a big old knotted lump of cancer inside it and not say anything – that's pretty. I mean, that's pretty big, isn't it? Never thought I'd be able for something like that but… it's amazing the things you can *not* say to someone – when they're in the bed beside you. It's amazing the things you can keep to yourself.

Beat.

I'm sort of proud of myself. In a way. For that. Didn't think I had it in me.

GAIL *doesn't know how to respond.*

Anyway. Sorry for – opening the floodgates. Thank God it was you and not some… total stranger.

GAIL. Why don't you sit down? Let me get us a drink or –

LAURA *looks at the tissue, moves away.*

LAURA. We should probably get on.

GAIL. Get on?

LAURA. Don't want to waste your morning.

GAIL. You're not wasting my /

LAURA. You've got your big day – your big meeting. About your book.

GAIL. Well, yes but –

LAURA. Let's just get on with it.

GAIL. It just seems like – under the circumstances, it might be a bit… you know to just to – you might not feel – after – you might not feel so – Moulin Rouge.

LAURA. No, I do. I do. I do. I feel totally – Moulin Rouge. I'm all over the Moulin Rouge.

LAURA *does a half-hearted little Moulin Rouge type of gesture.*

GAIL. Because we can always do this some other day.

LAURA. Well, we probably can't because I've work and there'll be bandages –

GAIL. What I mean is – there's no rush.

LAURA. His birthday's Saturday.

GAIL. I'm sure you could find him something else. Does he like football?

LAURA. I *want* to do this.

GAIL. Okay.

LAURA. I want to be able to do this.

GAIL. Sure. I – yeah. Alright.

LAURA. I'll just give my face a bit of a freshen-up and then we'll – rock and roll.

LAURA *goes behind the screen.* GAIL *stands in the room, rattled. The shadow of Sarah appears on the muslin cloth. A second woman appears beside her.*

LAURA comes back out with her make-up bag and a compact mirror. She notices GAIL *watching the two women.*

Who's your woman?

The women move away. LAURA *goes to the stool.* GAIL *stays staring at the muslin.*

GAIL. What?

LAURA. The second shadow puppet? Out there with Sarah?

GAIL. Em. She's – a friend. Of Sarah's.

LAURA *starts fixing her face.*

LAURA. Oh. Right. I hate puppets, don't you?

GAIL. They're sleeping together.

LAURA *looks at* GAIL.

LAURA. What?

GAIL. Sarah and that – woman in the hall. They're – sleeping together.

LAURA. Sleeping together?

GAIL. I feel sick.

LAURA. Are you okay?

GAIL. No.

LAURA. No?

GAIL. I mean, yes. I just… hadn't expected to see that. Like that. Now. After you just –

LAURA *points to the stool.*

LAURA. Do you want to sit down?

GAIL. I don't think so.

LAURA. Are you going to cry?

GAIL. I don't think so.

LAURA. You look like you might.

GAIL. I might.

LAURA. Sit down.

> GAIL *sits, takes a breath.*

GAIL. This is ridiculous. I shouldn't be – I knew they were in there.

LAURA. You knew they were in there?

GAIL. Sarah told me this morning. She came into my room especially – to say they had been out last night and they came back here. She told me so I wouldn't be surprised – but I still hadn't expected to – *see* it. Myself. With my own eyes, you know.

LAURA. Sarah and the other woman?

GAIL. Yes, Sarah and the other woman.

LAURA. That she's sleeping with?

GAIL. Hmmn.

> *Beat.*

LAURA. And are you – okay with Sarah… sleeping with that other woman?

GAIL. Okay?

LAURA. Like, is it something you've – agreed to between yourselves?

> GAIL *looks at* LAURA, *tries to regain composure.*

GAIL. No. Jesus, no. Of course not.

LAURA. Sorry. I just. The way you just said they're sleeping together like it was – I thought maybe – it was fine. In a bohemian kind of way.

GAIL. No, it's not. It is not – fine. We're not fine. Me and Sarah are not – together. Any more.

LAURA. Oh.

> *Beat.*

I'm a bit confused.

GAIL. I told you I wasn't the person to be handing out 'tips'.

LAURA. So you're not with Sarah?

GAIL. No.

LAURA. But you *were* with Sarah? For ten years?

GAIL. We finished it. A few weeks back. When Sarah came home and told me she was in love with somebody else. That woman, in fact, in the hallway.

LAURA. Oh.

GAIL. Yes.

LAURA. That's horrific.

GAIL. Well, no. It's not horrific. You have cancer – that's horrific, this hardly compares to /

LAURA. Well, not much compares to cancer. Really. Cancer's a bit of a trump card. When you want to silence the table – whip out an old 'I've got cancer' story. Works every time. It's still…

GAIL. Yeah.

LAURA. Yeah.

Beat.

GAIL. She's another doctor. That woman in the hallway. That Sarah's in love with. They met at a conference. A month ago… But they know.

LAURA. They know what?

GAIL. That it's love. They just *know*. (*Raising her voice slightly.*) Even though they only met each other *a month ago*.

LAURA. You poor love.

GAIL. I'm fine. I'm just – that just – caught me off-guard. But I'm fine.

LAURA. So you – broke up a month ago with Sarah?

GAIL. Yes.

LAURA. But you're still – living in this apartment with Sarah?

GAIL. Yes.

LAURA. Shouldn't you move out?

GAIL. I can't afford to move out.

LAURA. Shouldn't she move out?

GAIL. Well, yes, she should. Technically, *she* should but she's sort of… well, she's sort of paying for me to stay. She's sort of paying the whole mortgage.

LAURA. Oh.

GAIL. Until things pick up. And we know about the book.

LAURA. Right.

GAIL. I'm in the room with the furniture. So many levels of resentment.

Beat.

GAIL *looks at* LAURA.

So, not quite the roaring school success story after all.

LAURA. No, of course you are – you are – it's just… shite.

GAIL. Ten years. You know, it does sort of make me wish we'd had a wedding. At least then I could have cut up her dress. Or my dress. Or done something irredeemably – vengeful. You should definitely have a wedding. A really fucking huge one that costs an obscene amount of money – so everyone has to give you great presents. You can do some seriously good damage to wedding presents. Worst I've managed so far is to smash a coffee cup and de-friend her on Facebook. When did heartbreak get so fucking tepid?

LAURA *doesn't know what to say.*

Another bloody doctor – how dull is that?

LAURA. Unspeakably dull. Can she – hear you?

GAIL. I hope so. Sarah likes art. Sarah likes photography. What are they going to do – take each other's temperature all day?

LAURA. Probably.

GAIL. Yeah, probably. I can't stand the thought of their love-making. Do you think it means more to her than ours did?

LAURA *opens her mouth, about to answer.* GAIL *cuts in.*

No. Don't – please – don't answer that. I'm just wallowing now.

GAIL *gets up and goes to her camera, but has one final thing to say.*

At least she didn't lie, you know. She told me to my face as soon as it – at least she was honest.

LAURA. Well /

GAIL. Can I be honest with you, Laura?

LAURA. Me?

GAIL. I don't think the Moulin Rouge look really suits you.

LAURA. Oh.

GAIL. Or the Guinevere look for that matter.

LAURA. Right.

GAIL. I'm sorry. That came out a bit – but you said earlier I was the one person you knew wouldn't blow smoke up your –

LAURA. No. Yeah. It's – it's just a – bit of a sudden change of topic there, but it's alright.

GAIL. I can see what you're trying to do with it and I think it's a very – original idea, but from a professional standpoint I'm not sure it's going to work.

LAURA. No?

GAIL. I mean – yes, if we had a make-up artist and a hair person and a professional stylist – but we're just you and me and this little studio. In my living room. With a bag of clothes. I think we're going to have to – I think we're going to have to think less big-budget Hollywood and more… low-budget indie. If these are going to look as good as you want them.

LAURA. Low-budget indie?

GAIL. Yes.

LAURA. What does that mean?

GAIL. It means we'll have to strip things back.

LAURA. Right.

GAIL. And I was wondering, Laura, if… that was sort of the point?

LAURA *looks at* GAIL *a little blankly.*

I mean, I don't want to make any assumptions here and correct me if I'm wrong but… I was just wondering if – perhaps – if – when you get right down to it – that was the reason you came here today. To me.

LAURA. … To – strip things back?

GAIL. It's understandable. Given what you're going through. Given the treatment – it's more than understandable. And I can see why you'd want a friendly face. To do it. You say it's not a drastic operation but it's an operation and it's cancer. If it were my breasts, I'd probably want some pictures. I mean, I remember in school when your mother – I never even said I was sorry for your loss. And I was sorry for your loss – I am sorry – I was just… You can tell me. You can be frank. Is that what's really going on under all this – Fossett's Circus stuff?

LAURA. Fossett's Circus?

GAIL. You know what I mean.

LAURA. Is that what I look like? Something out of Fossett's Circus?

GAIL. No, I just meant –

LAURA. Oh my God.

LAURA *looks stricken.*

GAIL. I just meant it's a costume. It's an outfit. And – well, don't you think Simon would prefer something a bit more – authentic – than an outfit. Don't you think that – once he knows – once you tell him, he might appreciate something a bit more – you?

LAURA. I don't know.

GAIL. I've shot plenty of nudes before, Laura, I know what I'm doing.

LAURA. No, what I mean is – I don't know if I will tell him. Simon. Ever.

GAIL. What do you mean?

LAURA. I mean… if I give Simon a picture of me – naked for his birthday and then I go and tell him I have cancer, isn't that like – isn't that like I'm asking him to say goodbye to my body?

GAIL. No –

LAURA. I don't want to say goodbye to my body.

GAIL. That's not what I /

LAURA. So why would I want him to say goodbye to my body. I want to be sexy. I want to be strong. I want to be the woman he bought this corset for – I don't want to be my mother lying in a box. And if I don't tell him, he won't know –

GAIL. Laura. He's going to find out eventually.

LAURA. Not if I leave him.

GAIL. Leave him?

Beat.

LAURA. The thing you need to understand is – I didn't think I'd meet a man like Simon. I didn't think I'd meet anyone, to be honest. I hit thirty-five. And I thought – that's it, I'm done. I'm not even looking any more because it's never going to happen. I'm just one of those people. I'm just one of those people who is meant to be on their own and that's fine. I like my job, I have my friends – who needs a fella? And then – out of the blue, Simon. And he's great. And we fall in love and he wants to marry me and spend the rest of his life with me and it's like – it's like every fucking fairytale you've ever bloody read. It's like happily-ever-after multiplied by ten – because Simon's a good man. He really is. If I tell him, he'll be fantastic. He'll drive me to radiotherapy, he'll help me change bandages, he'll bring me breakfast in bed – but he'll be doing it knowing I've a lump in my breast. He'll be doing it knowing I've cancer.

GAIL. Yes, but /

LAURA. And even though I love all these – stories about Guinevere and Medb and what have you – I've never wanted anyone to rescue me. Not like that. Not from cancer. So I figure if I do this photo album and I give him a great birthday – a birthday he can never forget and then I end it – cleanly – before they take me into hospital next week… Things can stay just the way they are. Now. Before it all gets – (*She gestures to the hall.*) broken.

Beat.

And then I'll always get to be the woman he bought this corset for. And I'd like that. I'd like to – know that.

Beat.

I don't want to look like something out of a circus, though.

GAIL. Well – no. Yes. Okay. That's… well, what about that?

GAIL *points to the long red dress.*

Found it in your bag. It's not Moulin Rouge, but it's… nice.

LAURA. Yeah. That one was supposed to be for a jazz singer. There was this one story on the blog about this singer in a red silk dress who could seduce whole crowds with her voice. All she had to do was stand up and sing and she could make entire audiences fall violently in love with her. It was her gift in a way. Cos even though it only lasted the length of her song… for those few minutes everyone in the room knew what it felt like to be madly in love.

She smiles.

I thought maybe – we could get a picture of me in the dress on a grand piano. Sort of swinging my legs over the keys and throwing my head back. I thought that would look – quite good.

GAIL. It would – look quite good.

LAURA. Only – I don't know where we're going to get a grand piano… You don't have one here by any chance?

GAIL. No.

LAURA. I really should've planned this better.

Outside in the hall, a woman is silhouetted as she puts on a coat. On the muslin cloth the shadow of the second woman appears and puts her arm around the first woman, maybe fixes her scarf. It's tender and intimate. GAIL *watches.* LAURA *watches* GAIL.

Are they doing that on purpose?

GAIL. I think they've just forgotten that I'm here.

LAURA. They should have some compassion. They're doctors. No wonder our healthcare is fucked.

GAIL *keeps watching the scene.* LAURA *keeps watching* GAIL.

You'll meet someone else, you know. You will. Give it time. In a few months – in a few months you won't remember what this even felt like. It'll be a distant memory… like – school.

LAURA *looks at the dress.*

I'll give this a try, so. Maybe we don't need the piano. Maybe we can… Will you – would you give me a hand with these laces? Never can undo the bloody things myself.

LAURA *turns and presents* GAIL *with the back of her corset. The silhouettes in the hall move off, as* GAIL *methodically unlaces* LAURA.

Fade.

TWO

The back room of a funeral parlour in South County Dublin.

Afternoon.

In the centre of the room is a coffin. The body of JOE's *mother is laid out.*

The body is somewhat raised inside, and the clasped white hands of the corpse with a set of rosary beads interlaced between the fingers can be seen protruding a little over the top.

JOE *and* CARMEL *face the coffin solemnly.*

Silence.

JOE. This is a desperate business altogether.

CARMEL. I know.

JOE. I just can't get my head around it at all.

Beat.

Do you think…

CARMEL. What?

JOE. Ah. Nothing. Nothing. Forget it.

Beat. He looks at the body.

I just – I'd love to bate the head off her, that's all.

CARMEL. Joe /

JOE. I know it's a bit late now but – there it is.

CARMEL *takes a deep breath.*

Do you think she did it on purpose?

CARMEL. Of course she did it on purpose.

JOE. No, but. Do you think she did it – you know – to get at me in some way?

CARMEL. Come on.

JOE. As revenge.

CARMEL *shakes her head.*

CARMEL. That's just /

JOE. It's one way of getting someone's attention.

CARMEL. – silly, Joe.

JOE. No, but she could've.

CARMEL. It had nothing to do with you.

JOE. You're sure?

CARMEL. I could start torturing myself like that too if I wanted.

JOE. Yeah, no. I know. I know that.

Beat.

They look at the coffin.

JOE *gets up in frustration and maybe kicks something nearby.*

Ah, for fuck's sake.

CARMEL. Keep your voice down, Joe.

JOE. Of all the frigging things to do to a person.

CARMEL. There are other people here too.

JOE. It's completely fucking ungrateful. And – and selfish and just downright idiotic. Don't you think?

CARMEL. Yes.

JOE. Up on the internet. The internet. That girl has a degree from Trinity College, for God's sake, and this is how she shows her intelligence to the world.

CARMEL. Look, this is what happens, they go off for one year and they –

JOE. Forget their sense of decency.

CARMEL. Lose their inhibitions.

JOE. You can say that again.

CARMEL. It's all the relief after all that pressure. She knows you're disappointed.

JOE. Disappointed? I'm fecking – she's lucky she's in Australia, that's all I'll say.

CARMEL. Joe, there's a family next door.

JOE. And my mother lying here cold.

CARMEL. I know.

JOE. It's a desperate state of affairs.

Silence.

JOE *looks at the coffin. He shakes his head.* CARMEL *leans in to look at the corpse.*

CARMEL. She looks good, doesn't she?

JOE. Hmmmnn.

CARMEL. Pretty. I like what they've done with her hair.

JOE. She'd have hated it.

CARMEL. I think it makes her face look slimmer.

JOE. Her face looks slimmer cos she's dead, Carmel. It's a little late for the weight-loss techniques.

CARMEL. That's a terrible way to talk.

JOE. What time will the others get here?

CARMEL. I don't know. Five-ish?

JOE. Well, what are we doing here so?

CARMEL. Joe, this is the last time you are going to see her alone – forget about Emer for five minutes.

JOE *looks into the coffin.*

JOE. You're right. No, you're right.

Beat.

It's weird, isn't it? I'm an orphan now.

CARMEL. Hmmnn.

JOE. My very first memory is of her buttoning up my duffel coat in the hall before school. In winter she used make us all wear these itchy friggin' balaclavas over our heads that got us beaten up the minute we walked through the school gates. She meant well, but it was a terrible cruelty to visit on your own children. I can still see her there in her flowery pinafore thing waving us all off from the doorway.

CARMEL. That's nice.

JOE. She was a great mystery to me in those days. Always wondered what she did when she closed the door, you know. I imagined she was having a very glamorous time of it, reading magazines and having baths while we slaved away under the Christian Brothers. But sure, she probably wasn't. The poor auld thing. She probably – wasn't.

He leans over and affectionately puts a hand over the corpse's hand.

Little did she know that one day her heritage would lead her to be the proud grandmother of an internet trollop.

CARMEL. Joe, for God's sake –

JOE. She didn't even offer to come home when I told her.

CARMEL. That's because of what you said.

JOE. What did I say?

CARMEL. 'I hope you're happy you've finally killed your grandmother.'

JOE. I didn't say that.

CARMEL. I was standing beside you.

JOE. Well, she did, didn't she?

CARMEL. She did not. For goodness' sake, your mother didn't know anything about it.

JOE. Thank Christ.

CARMEL. Why would you say a thing like that to someone who's in shock?

JOE. She's not in shock. Emer is not in shock. She's over there in Australia getting drunk and taking her clothes off and posting the pictures up on the internet – is that your idea of shock?

CARMEL. She's upset, Joe, the same as all of us. It's her granny.

JOE *snorts*.

There would have been no point of her coming all the way home for the funeral.

JOE. A gesture would've been nice.

CARMEL. Do you know what you're doing here now?

JOE. What?

CARMEL. You're projecting.

JOE. How's that?

CARMEL. Because you're grieving. Because it's easier to work yourself up about a few pictures of your daughter than it is to face the fact that your mother is dead.

JOE. Is that right?

CARMEL. Yes.

JOE. And since when did you become the state psychologist?

CARMEL. What does that mean?

JOE. Thinking you know everything about everyone.

CARMEL. There's no state psychologist /

JOE. Thinking you can get into people's heads.

CARMEL. There's a state pathologist, is that what you meant?

JOE. I'm upset about Emer because I'm upset about Emer. It's nothing to do with my mother.

CARMEL. Fine.

Beat.

CARMEL *looks at the lilies in the corner.*

This place is alright, isn't it?

JOE. What do you mean?

CARMEL. It has a sort of a – warmish feel to it. For a funeral home.

JOE. I suppose.

CARMEL. I thought it would be much grimmer.

JOE. Are we making small talk here? Is that what we're doing?

CARMEL. I'm just /

JOE. Cos I'm not really in the mood for small talk, Carmel.

CARMEL. I'm just waiting for you to say whatever you want to say.

JOE. I want to say that I am absolutely enraged /

CARMEL. To your mother. I'm waiting for you to say whatever you have to say to her.

JOE. I've nothing to say to her.

CARMEL. Would you like me to wait outside?

JOE. Why?

CARMEL. So you can have some privacy.

JOE. No.

CARMEL. Are you sure?

JOE. Yes, I'm sure.

> JOE *paces a bit and turns back to have a look at his mother.* CARMEL *looks at her hand.*

CARMEL. Emer gave her those rosary beads, you know.

JOE. When?

CARMEL. When she and I went to Rome that time. She bought them at the Vatican shop. They'd loads of different ones, but Emer picked those because they were feminine. I paid for them, but Emer picked them and it's the thought that matters. They were very close, your mother and Emer.

JOE. Brought together by religion no doubt.

>   JOE *thinks about that*. CARMEL *looks at the body*.

CARMEL. She was very attractive, really – for a woman who had six children.

JOE. Oh, she was a stunner. In her day – an absolute – She could've had her pick of the men of Rialto.

CARMEL. I wonder what attracted her to your father.

JOE. Same thing that attracted you to me I'd say – a few bob.

CARMEL. Yeah right.

JOE. What does that mean?

CARMEL. Nothing.

JOE. And that's another thing, you know – something like that can have detrimental consequences on employment opportunities. The internet is the first place they go nowadays to check on the sort of people they're hiring. If they find pictures like that –

CARMEL. They're not going to find them.

JOE. They might.

CARMEL. I don't even know how you managed to find them. Don't you need an account to access that sort of thing?

JOE. She has one of them – open profiles.

CARMEL. And what were you doing looking at it?

JOE. I came across it.

CARMEL. You 'came across it'?

JOE. It's the internet, Carmel. You can stumble across all sorts of disgusting and perverted things on it without knowing how you got there.

CARMEL. It was hardly disgusting and perverted. It was a wet T-shirt /

JOE. It's a moral-free zone. There's no policing on there. Anyone could see those pictures – my brothers, their wives.

Beat.

Jesus. Do you think my brothers and their wives have seen them?

CARMEL. No.

JOE. You're looking at me like I've done something wrong by finding them. Sure, at least now – we can put a stop to it. I've told her in no uncertain terms. She might think twice about doing something like that again.

CARMEL. She might. But you know, there's also a chance that she may not. Because, let's face it, Joe, they're a different generation and things like this aren't really such a big deal to them. And as pictures go – I have to say – they weren't really too bad.

JOE. What?

JOE stares at CARMEL in disbelief.

CARMEL. I was expecting a lot worse.

JOE. How could they have been any worse?

CARMEL. They were only having a bit of fun. They're on holidays. And, you know, in a way, looking at them, I was sort of – proud.

JOE. Proud?

CARMEL. In a way.

JOE. In what way?

CARMEL. She has a nice figure.

JOE. What?

CARMEL. I'd like to think that she gets it from me.

JOE. Are you out of your mind? Here's me trying to discipline the wretch and you're there saying you're proud of her.

CARMEL. I didn't say it to her.

JOE. She's underage, Carmel.

CARMEL. She's twenty-two and she was with her friends /

JOE. So what – I should reward her?

CARMEL. No.

JOE. Will I send her some early birthday money?

CARMEL. That is not what I'm /

JOE. I know, maybe we could buy her one of them steel poles for Christmas and she can make a bit of money twisting and gyrating on it for the punters. They can throw coins. It'll be her new party piece at family gatherings. That'll put her degree to good use.

He leans into the coffin.

What do you think about that idea, Ma? An old pole?

CARMEL. Joe, that's horrible /

JOE. That's your granddaughter we're talking about.

JOE *steps back suddenly.*

Jesus.

CARMEL. What is it?

JOE. I thought I just saw her wink.

CARMEL. What?

JOE. I got this sudden flash, you know.

CARMEL. Of her winking?

JOE. She had that little tic remember? In her left eye?

CARMEL. No.

JOE. You do. It would go all funny whenever one of us said something she didn't like. It was kind of a wink. But – more sinister.

CARMEL. A sinister wink?

JOE. Sort of, yeah. God, I hated that wink. She seemed to aim it at me more than any of the rest of them. I'm very glad I won't have to see that wink again I can tell you.

He shivers and walks away.

Beat.

CARMEL *watches him closely.*

CARMEL. Do you think she was particularly hard on you?

JOE. Huh?

CARMEL. Your mother. Do you think she was harder on you than she was – say – on the others? You've always talked about her like she was.

JOE. Ah now. It's not nice to talk ill of the dead.

CARMEL. I'm not talking ill of her. I'm just asking.

JOE. Well, you shouldn't.

CARMEL. It's just you and me here, Joe. This is an opportunity.

JOE. For what?

CARMEL. If there's anything you feel you – want to get out or that you… needed to say to her in life that you maybe didn't – have the guts to –

JOE. What do you mean 'didn't have the guts'?

CARMEL. Not 'didn't have the guts' /

JOE. Do you think I was afraid of her?

CARMEL. Yes, a bit.

JOE. What?

CARMEL. Most men are afraid of their mothers, Joe. It's very common.

JOE. She was a little old lady, Carmel. For God's sake, look at her, she's hardly Count Dracula.

CARMEL. She was the most powerful presence in your life for your most formative years, it gave her a lot of control.

JOE. You've lost the plot.

CARMEL. She was a tough woman, Joe, we both know that. From our wedding day to the Christmas dinner, she ran every family get-together with an iron fist.

JOE. I'm not afraid of her, Carmel.

CARMEL. I'm just asking – did she ever make you feel – bad about yourself? Or – I don't know – ashamed in some way?

JOE. No. She was a wonderful mother. (*To the corpse.*) You were a great mother, Ma. See, I said something to her?

CARMEL. What about the winking?

JOE. The winking? What are you – the winking was nothing. I was only saying.

CARMEL. You were only saying what?

JOE. It was a throwaway comment.

CARMEL. It didn't seem throwaway.

JOE. Well, it was. Ma, if you're listening, the winking wasn't important. I didn't like it, but I could live with it. You were a great mother and you were very fair and – don't listen to her. She's in a strange mood. (*To* CARMEL.) Would you give over now with this touchy-feely nonsense? You're making my chest hurt.

   CARMEL *relents silently.* JOE *loosens his tie.*

   Who's paid for all this anyway?

CARMEL. What?

JOE. This. Flowers, coffins, sandwiches. Have we paid for it?

CARMEL. Well, we've paid for it so far.

JOE. Have we? Did none of the others even offer to chip in?

CARMEL. Well /

JOE. Unbelievable. They all know about the business. You'd think they'd at least offer to put their hands in their pockets for their own mother.

CARMEL. I said that we'd wait until everything was done and then we could divide it by the six of you after.

JOE. That's ludicrous.

CARMEL. Do you want them to pay upfront?

JOE. Of course I don't want them to pay upfront. I don't want them paying for it at all, you shouldn't have even brought it up.

CARMEL. But /

JOE. I'll not be shown up in front of my own family, Carmel. I don't want them thinking we need handouts. I'm the eldest, they expect things. She expected things.

CARMEL. Did she? What did she expect?

JOE. She expected me to take care of things.

CARMEL. Well, that must have been a burden, all that expectation.

JOE. Look – don't start with this again. I'm just saying you're not to take a penny off anyone.

CARMEL. And what if they offer?

JOE. Not a penny. We're not a charity case. I can pay for a coffin. I'm not useless, you know.

He sits down.

They look at each other. They look at the body.

Beat.

CARMEL. You could give grinds.

JOE. Grinds?

CARMEL. Business studies.

JOE. What?

CARMEL. There must be loads of kids out there needing them. For the leaving cert or what have you –

JOE. What qualifications do I have to be giving grinds?

CARMEL. You ran your own business for twenty years. That's qualification enough.

JOE. It is not.

CARMEL. You'd just need one day with the textbook – it'd be a doddle. There's a woman in work whose son's in fifth year and he's really struggling. I said I'd ask you.

JOE. To do what?

CARMEL. Twenty euro an hour.

JOE. I can't take money off some poor woman for grinds, Carmel.

CARMEL. It'd get you out of the house.

JOE. Is that what this is about?

CARMEL. I think you'd be good at it.

JOE. You're unbelievable. *You* probably paid her, did you?

CARMEL. Of course I didn't.

JOE gets up and walks away.

I just – I don't think it's good for you this – being at home all the time. It doesn't suit your personality.

JOE. What's wrong with my personality?

CARMEL. It's making you anxious. It's making you – fixate on things.

JOE. Like what things?

CARMEL. Like Emer. Or your mother.

JOE. My mother just died.

CARMEL. A few grinds a week would be no harm.

JOE. Look, who put up those bookshelves you wanted? Who unblocked the drains? I hadn't time to do those things before but now…

He looks at his mother.

If you'd stayed alive another bit longer I could've helped
you with a few things too, Ma. That back patio for one.

CARMEL *gets up suddenly, looking upset.*

What's wrong with you?

CARMEL. Nothing.

JOE. You've gone all teary.

She turns away.

CARMEL. I haven't.

JOE. Now look, there's no need to – everything's going to be
fine. This is just a – a transitional phase until I make a few
decisions. Sure isn't half the country in the same boat? We'll
be okay.

CARMEL. I know that. I still have a job, remember.

JOE. Well, then.

She turns back to him suddenly.

CARMEL. If it were me, in that coffin, and not your mother,
would you be acting like this?

JOE. What?

CARMEL. If it were me – lying there – cold as ice in my
Sunday best – would you… would you have nothing to say
to me like you have nothing to say to her?

JOE. What Sunday best – ?

CARMEL. Or would you just be here with Emer, griping and
snarling at each other and watching the clock until it was
time to take me to the church?

JOE. What has gotten in to you?

CARMEL. I just want to know. If I were dead, would you be
rushing to bury me as fast as you could or would you by
some miracle want to use this time to – unburden your heart?

JOE. Unburden my –

CARMEL. I mean, death is death, Joe. If you can't say what you want to say to a person when they're dead, when can you say it?

JOE. You're not dead, Carmel.

CARMEL. I know.

JOE. So how the feck do I know what I'd be doing if you were?

CARMEL. Try to imagine.

JOE. I don't want to imagine. It isn't a nice thought. It's awful. And to be quite frank I think this is a bit – self-indulgent. Talking about yourself being dead and what I'd say to your corpse when my mother is lying in front of us and it's her we should be mourning. What are you like?

Beat.

CARMEL *gets up.*

CARMEL. You're right.

JOE. Course I'm right. Jesus.

CARMEL. What's the use of talking to someone when they're dead? It's in life we should be speaking to each other, isn't it?

She paces the room a little. JOE *watches, concerned.*

JOE. Is all this because of that – meditation group you've been going to on Wednesdays? Did they go putting ideas into your head? Angel cards, my balls. Those new-age places are all the same, Carmel. Sad, middle-aged women replacing sex with… fairies and stuff. You can't replace sex with fairies. All this navel gazing. It's not healthy. It's navel using they should be doing, what?

He laughs to himself. CARMEL *looks at him witheringly.*

Ah look, I'm trying to lighten the mood here. Jesus.

CARMEL. I think you're a hypocrite, Joe.

JOE. What?

CARMEL. Being angry at Emer, I think you are a complete and utter hypocrite. And I think you know you're a hypocrite too. Which is why you're so angry.

JOE. What's gotten in to you?

CARMEL starts searching in her handbag.

CARMEL. So she put a few pictures up on some website. It wasn't like she – I don't know – tried to make some money out of it or something.

JOE. Money? What are you on about?

She holds up a pair of stockings.

CARMEL. What are these, Joe?

JOE. What?

CARMEL. What. Are. These?

JOE looks at the corpse, then back at CARMEL.

JOE. Have I – is this – am I actually standing in a room with my mother's corpse while my wife holds up a pair of her tights?

CARMEL. They're not tights, Joe. They're stockings. And they're not mine.

JOE. …Well, whose are they?

CARMEL. Yours.

JOE. Mine? Jesus, Carmel. That's – now that is just the straw that broke the camel's – you've lost the run of yourself completely.

CARMEL. They came in the post.

JOE. Post?

CARMEL. In an envelope addressed to you. When you were at the hospital with your mother.

JOE. And what – you think that makes them mine?

CARMEL. Who else's would they be?

JOE. …What the hell would I be doing buying tights, Carmel?

CARMEL. Stockings.

JOE. What would I be doing buying stockings?

CARMEL. That's what I'm asking you.

JOE. It's a mistake, Carmel – any eejit could see that. It's a mix-up, they must have been – I don't know – sent to the wrong house or something.

CARMEL. You think?

JOE. Of course I do. Jesus.

CARMEL. It just… there was a receipt inside the envelope, Joe. With your credit-card number on it.

JOE. What?

CARMEL hands him a receipt. He looks at it.

CARMEL. Although I'm not sure how much credit you have on the thing considering it's me that pays it off every month.

JOE. Well, that's… that's a complete disgrace. I'll have to get onto the bank. They're always sending me stuff about online fraud and – here – here we've a perfect example of it.

CARMEL. There was also a compliment slip.

She looks inside the bag again for the compliment slip.

JOE. Huh?

CARMEL. From a girl called Abbi.

JOE. Abbi?

CARMEL. Abbi. Has her own website. Turns out she does a roaring trade selling her knickers on it.

JOE. Carmel.

CARMEL. Not just knickers – stockings, bras, basques, whatever. The whole lot. The ultimate selling-point being – of course – that she's worn them already.

JOE. Carmel, I have no idea who this Abbi –

She fishes out a pink compliments slip.

CARMEL. 'Dear Joe, have fun with these little naughties, I know I did. Love, Abbi.' A-B-B-I. Heart over the i.

JOE *looks at her helplessly.*

JOE. Carmel –

CARMEL. Do you want a sniff?

JOE. No, I don't want a sniff.

CARMEL. Have a sniff.

JOE. No.

CARMEL. It's what you paid for.

JOE. I did not – pull yourself together, Carmel, for God's sake.

CARMEL. Pull *myself* together?

JOE. This is hardly the time or the place to be having. Those – things are nothing to do with me, I did not order those from –

CARMEL. Abbi –

JOE. And I have absolutely no idea who this –

CARMEL. Abbi –

JOE. I have no idea who she is.

CARMEL. Joe /

JOE. And I might ask you, Carmel – what the hell you were doing going and opening my post in the first place?

CARMEL. Oh, I see. That's the problem here, is it? Me opening your post?

JOE. Yes – actually. It is.

CARMEL. The worry here is that I opened a letter addressed to you not that you ordered a pair of stockings for yourself from a girl called Abbi?

JOE. I did not and I will not – be accused. You had no right to – invade my privacy like that, Carmel. No right.

CARMEL. Even though you don't know anything about this Abbi?

JOE. Yes. It's the principle. Opening other people's letters – whether they're theirs – or someone else's – is actually an illegal thing to do. You've committed an offence doing that, you know. You could be put in jail.

CARMEL. Jail.

JOE. Yes.

CARMEL. My husband receives a package in a pink envelope reeking of perfume and I'm expected not to bat an eyelid, am I?

JOE. I don't like the idea that my – personal property – even if it isn't mine – means so little to you, Carmel. I don't like that at all.

CARMEL *stares at him.*

That's a very – disturbing thing you did. Opening that letter, that's a very unsettling – I mean, I don't – you shouldn't have – I'm angry about that, Carmel, actually – I really am.

CARMEL. Oh, come off it, Joe.

JOE. No – I'm pissed off with you. That's just – that just beggars belief.

He looks at her. She looks at him.

CARMEL. Maybe I opened it by mistake.

JOE. Well… that's no excuse.

CARMEL. Maybe I thought that the pink envelope and the pretty writing meant it was for me. Maybe it was an accident I opened it, Joe.

JOE. Was it an accident?

CARMEL. No, it wasn't a fucking accident, I tore the damn thing open the second I laid eyes on it and stood staring in what I can only describe as pure disbelief at a pair of – used stockings – wondering if the moment had finally arrived when I'd have to confront my husband about being a cross-dresser.

JOE. Ah Jesus. I'm not a cross-dresser –

CARMEL. No, sadly not. You're just an ordinary pervert.

JOE. I told you there's been a mix-up – someone must've taken my credit-card number.

CARMEL. No one took your credit-card number. And the sooner you stop lying and tell me the truth the better. You bought them, didn't you, Joe?

JOE. No.

CARMEL. Tell me the truth.

JOE. I am telling you the truth. Will you stop waving those things in my face?

CARMEL. For the last time, Joe.

JOE. This is entirely inappropriate. This is a funeral home, Carmel. There are people here.

CARMEL *laughs bitterly.*

CARMEL. Now he cares –

JOE. These are my last few minutes alone with my mother.

CARMEL. A moment ago you had nothing to say to her.

JOE. Look –

CARMEL. I need to believe that you are a better man than I currently believe you to be, Joe.

JOE. Carmel –

CARMEL. I need to believe that you are capable of being honest, if not with your mother then at least with me.

JOE. That is not fair.

CARMEL. So for the last time, Joe – the truth. Did you or did you not purchase these stockings using the credit card that I pay for from somebody called Abbi who dots her i's with hearts?

Beat.

JOE....No.

They look at each other.

CARMEL. I see.

CARMEL folds the stockings up.

She carefully walks towards JOE. *She looks at him.*

Suddenly she kicks him in the shin.

He stumbles backwards in agony.

JOE. For fuck's sake, Carmel, Jesus.

CARMEL. You're a liar.

JOE. That's my weak leg.

CARMEL. And a hypocrite.

JOE. Christ.

He stands up. She looks at him.

Okay, alright. I bought them. I bought the stockings but I can explain.

CARMEL. Explain.

JOE (*re: the leg*). Fucking hell. It was… a joke.

CARMEL. A joke?

JOE. A mistake. The stockings – they were a mistake. I didn't mean to buy them.

CARMEL. You didn't mean to buy them?

JOE. No, okay. Look. I bought them. I bought the stockings, I did. And that doesn't look great.

CARMEL. No.

JOE. And I'm – I'm sorry, okay. I'm sorry that I bought them and that you found them – like that. But it isn't what you – I didn't mean to buy them – I mean, I did – mean to buy them and I admit that I bought them but it wasn't… for the reasons that you think.

CARMEL. What reasons do I think?

JOE. Well, you know. What you said before. About them being worn and stuff. It seems sort of kinky.

CARMEL. Yes it does.

JOE. But it's not.

CARMEL. It's not?

JOE. That's not what I was buying them for.

CARMEL. You were buying them for – non-kinky reasons?

JOE. Yes.

CARMEL. Like drying the dishes?

JOE. Ah, look /

CARMEL. Using as curtains?

JOE. You're taking this completely the wrong /

CARMEL. What, Joe?

JOE. It was just a bit of –

CARMEL. …

JOE. I thought it would be funny.

CARMEL. Funny?

JOE. I was looking on the internet one day and I came across
her – website and I thought it was a laugh. I was…

CARMEL. Curious?

JOE. Exactly, I was curious. They're just a pair of stockings,
Carmel. I mean, I know it seems… but really – when you get
down to it there's nothing in it. I was just – I was just a bit
bored. That's all.

CARMEL. Bored?

JOE. Yeah.

CARMEL. I see.

JOE. I didn't think it was a big deal.

CARMEL. So, what about the e-mails?

JOE. What – e-mails?

CARMEL. The ones in your inbox.

She takes out some paper.

From girls with names like Sandy or Suki or Sally, with e-mail addresses like sallylikesitgoodand underscore at eircom dot net.

JOE. What the –

CARMEL. What about those? Were those the result of a bit of afternoon boredom too?

JOE. Carmel, this is getting out of –

CARMEL. And before you start your whole 'invasion of privacy' speech again – the answer is yes. Yes, I did guess your password and yes, I did break into your e-mails and yes, I did read every single one of them behind your back and to be quite frank with you, Joe, I think that after the whole stockings debacle any lawyer in the land would say I had a pretty good case.

JOE. Carmel /

CARMEL. Here, I printed them off.

JOE. Oh God /

CARMEL. Sally – of the underscore – wants to rub sandpaper up and down your – manhood, according to this. Suki, God love her, just wants to sit on your face. How very vanilla.

JOE. Okay, stop it.

CARMEL. Although I think she does have something in mind with a leather belt and a blindfold.

JOE. Carmel /

CARMEL. Somewhere. Let me check that for you.

JOE. No.

CARMEL. One of them definitely mentioned it – yes. Here.

He lunges to grab the e-mails.

JOE. For fuck's sake, Carmel, what are you trying to do to me?

She holds them away.

My brothers will be here any minute.

CARMEL. And that's what you're worried about? That your brothers and your dead mother and the people next door might find out that you have an erotic affinity to DIY materials.

JOE. No.

CARMEL. What about your wife, Joe?

JOE. They're just – a few e-mails, Carmel. They don't mean anything. I was never going to actually – do anything.

CARMEL. Weren't you?

JOE. Of course I wasn't. Jesus. I'm a married man. They do this sort of thing for fun, these women. They write e-mails to men like me for a laugh – it's harmless stuff. Really. In a way. They're probably at work or something.

CARMEL. You say it like you haven't got anything to do with it. You say it like these e-mails were sent to you against your will.

JOE. Well, no. Okay, they weren't sent to me against my – but… they were just meant to – I never intended to – I don't even know what these women look like.

CARMEL. So how do you know they're women?

JOE. What?

CARMEL. Abbi sells her knickers on a website. We have no idea who she really is. Abbi could be a forty-year-old fat man trying to make a quick buck in a troubled economic climate.

JOE. Carmel /

CARMEL. Abbi could be a lad with a hairy chest who has bought a bulk of lacy knickers at the cash-and-carry.

JOE. Please.

CARMEL. Abbi's real name could be Dermot or Pedro or Gearóid.

JOE. Her name is not Gearóid.

CARMEL. Not quite such a saucy little minx now, eh?

JOE. Carmel, okay. Alright. I understand that you're angry. If the situation were reversed I'd be angry, I'd be fecking – furious but I don't think we can have this conversation now.

CARMEL. If your mother hadn't been dying, Joe, we could've had it a lot sooner. Do you think it has been easy keeping this in?

JOE. No, I don't. But please. Can we just take stock for one minute?

CARMEL. Posting underwear to married men is hardly the work of an empowered individual. These could belong to anyone – an immigrant forced over here by war and deprivation, a drug addict desperate for money –

JOE. Now look – you can't say – I mean, you can't know that any of these women –

CARMEL. If they are women /

JOE. Are – victims. Some of them might want to do it.

CARMEL. And that makes it okay?

JOE. No but – like you're saying – you're saying that I'm funding some sort of – I mean. You're saying that in buying these I'm colluding with desperate people.

CARMEL. Aren't you?

JOE. No. It's not like it's hardcore pornography. I mean, yes – I have come across some stuff – which I turned off immediately but… like, there's this one woman who writes kinky versions of myths and things. She has a whole fan club and her use of language and her imagery, I mean – she's definitely not some poor – she's probably a university professor over there in New York or somewhere.

CARMEL. What?

JOE. A lot of them are, these – blogging types. A lot of them are very intelligent, educated, sexually liberated women who just don't want their identities revealed.

CARMEL. What sort of twisted male fantasy-land are you living in, Joe? I doubt very much these came from the drawer of a university professor. More likely they belong to some girl no older than Emer –

JOE. Okay, stop. Let's not bring Emer into this, Emer is a separate issue –

CARMEL. Emer had the decency to own up to her mistake. Emer's not going around writing e-mails to strangers – telling them she's a big-shot businessman.

JOE. I never said that.

CARMEL. Oh no? Suki seems to think it. Suki seems to be under the misguided impression the bulge in your wallet matches the bulge in your trousers.

JOE. Well, I was hardly going to say that the business had collapsed. That's not very sexy, is it? Oh – Jesus that sounds fucking desperate.

CARMEL. Sandpaper, Joe. That sounds fucking desperate. That's just pathetic.

JOE *tries to walk away.*

JOE. I can't go into this any more, Carmel. I just can't. Not here.

CARMEL. What is it with the sandpaper anyway?

JOE. I mean it – I don't want herself being – privy to this.

CARMEL. Because that sounds pretty agonising to me.

JOE. What do I have to say, Carmel? What do I have to do?

CARMEL. Am I too gentle, is that the problem?

JOE. No.

CARMEL. Are my loving hands too soft to the touch? Would you rather I gave your scrotum a good hard squeeze because I tell you, Joe, that wouldn't be a problem now. I could squeeze the whole thing right off.

JOE. Alright. I'm going to get down on my knees.

He gets on his knees.

CARMEL. Oh, for God's sake.

JOE. No, I'm doing it /

CARMEL. Get up.

JOE. I'm on my knees. Here I am. On my knees. I've done a terrible foolish thing, Carmel. I admit it. I should never have gone and bought those – stockings and I should never have written to those women. It was wrong and I – shouldn't have done it.

He looks at her. Silence.

CARMEL. Oh, well then. Sure that's grand so.

JOE. No, it's not grand. It's not at all grand. And I'm sorry – I'm really sorry you had to open that package and I'm sorry you had to read those e-mails, Carmel, and I know – I know it's probably hard at the moment with the way you're feeling and all the emotions and – even though I never intended to do anything with these women – I can understand you're pretty raging right this minute but – (*Perhaps looking round to check on possible intruders.*) do you think there is any way we could talk about this when we're at home? You know when we're – alone and – not with her. And not in a place where people are saying their last goodbyes to their loved ones and not just before a load of my family turn up to offer their condolences? Do you think there is any way we could do that? Because, you know, I understand you're furious and I understand you want to have it out, but I have to say… I think all this is a bit – unseemly. Given the day that's in it. And herself being here. Dead. And all. You know?

Silence.

CARMEL *looks at him.*

Very slowly and without taking her eyes off JOE, *she folds the e-mails up and puts them in her bag.* JOE *watches.*

Thank you. Thanks, that's – thank – you.

JOE *gets up off the floor, wipes himself down.*

CARMEL *walks to the nearest chair, sits down and crosses her arms.*

JOE *takes a breath. He looks at* CARMEL. *She looks in the other direction.*

JOE *takes a few cautious steps in the direction of the door. He looks out. He looks back at* CARMEL, *then out again and slowly, he makes his way over to where she sits.*

JOE *very tentatively sits down on the chair next to her.* CARMEL *looks at her nails, then in the opposite direction.*

JOE *looks at his mother.*

Those are – they're lovely beads you and Emer bought her.

Silence.

It was probably more than she deserved.

CARMEL. Why do you say that?

JOE. Well – she could be an old dragon, I suppose, sometimes.

CARMEL *doesn't say anything.*

Not all the time, mind.

Beat.

But – sometimes.

Beat.

She wasn't always very nice to you, I know.

CARMEL. She was – fine.

JOE. No, but – like – she could be insensitive. With her comments. I do know that.

CARMEL. It's not nice to talk ill of the dead, Joe.

JOE. I know I never used to intervene and pull her up on it, even when she was… But like – what was the point? She was critical by nature. Always was. If I started getting defensive and telling her to stop talking that way about your curtains, or your legs or the way you made the dinner or whatever, sure, I'd never have heard the end of it.

CARMEL. What?

JOE. What?

CARMEL. What did she say about my legs?

JOE. Nothing. I just – that was just an example.

CARMEL *looks at the body.*

CARMEL. Did your mother used to criticise my legs?

JOE. No. She found fault with everything, absolutely everything, you know what she was like.

CARMEL. But... did she say something specifically about my legs?

JOE. No.

CARMEL. Joe.

JOE. She used. She used – sometimes – say things about them. Rarely though, really.

CARMEL. What sort of things did she used say?

JOE. Just stupid things.

CARMEL. Like?

JOE. Nothing important. Sure, she was always saying I had small ears.

CARMEL. What did she say to you about my legs?

JOE. She just said – she just – once – said that they were looking a bit on the heavy side that's all.

CARMEL. Are you making this up?

JOE. Why would I make it up?

CARMEL *glances down at her own legs.*

CARMEL. Your mother told you my legs were heavy behind my back?

JOE. She only said it once.

CARMEL. What else did she say about me?

JOE. Nothing. She – she was funny about most women.

CARMEL. You can say that again.

JOE. She only said it after you got the job in the bank. Before that, she always thought you took great care of yourself.

CARMEL. So what – I let myself go when I started working, is that it?

JOE. I don't know. This wasn't – I was only /

CARMEL. How dare she? How dare she say those things to you about your wife who earns her own living, who pays her own way –

JOE. She was old, Carmel. She was set in her ways.

CARMEL. No wonder you're so fucked up about women.

JOE. Ah now /

CARMEL. Off sleeping with strangers.

JOE. I'm not sleeping with anyone.

CARMEL. How do I know that?

JOE. Carmel, I have never been – unfaithful to you.

CARMEL. Except in your head.

JOE. Ah Jesus, I thought we weren't talking about this any more.

CARMEL. Well, we are. Because you have a problem.

JOE. For God's sake it's not like I've been going to see – prostitutes.

CARMEL. Do you think that would be worse?

JOE. I haven't done anything.

She pulls out the stockings.

CARMEL. What are these? Joe, once a man starts doing things like this – writing the sorts of e-mails you've been writing, visiting the sorts of websites you've been visiting, it's only a matter of time before he actually goes out and –

JOE. I have never cheated on you. Not once. They're just – they're just words. They're just e-mails.

CARMEL. Well, you don't write e-mails to me. Look, I've been speaking to someone about this.

JOE. What? Who?

CARMEL. A professional.

JOE. For fuck's sake, Carmel.

CARMEL. I was up the walls, Joe. I had to tell someone. And do you know what? It was very illuminating. I learned that it's a compulsion, this sort of thing. It's like gambling or drinking – you can't help yourself.

JOE. Ah now.

CARMEL. But there are twelve-step programmes /

JOE. I don't need a twelve-step programme.

CARMEL. So why did you keep it a secret?

JOE. A man has a right to his own mind, Carmel. Just because I'm your husband doesn't mean you own my thoughts. You can't know everything about me. I love you and we've been together twenty-four years and they've been mostly good but –

CARMEL. But what?

JOE. I know you inside out.

CARMEL. So – you're sick of me?

JOE. No.

CARMEL. You're bored? I don't do it for you any more?

JOE. Of course [not] – I love you, Carmel. I really do but you can't expect – I'm a human being. I have a right to my own... you know.

Beat.

CARMEL. Do you think you're the only person with fantasies in this marriage, Joe? Do you honestly think you're the only one of us who wouldn't mind a look around to see what else is out there?

JOE. Carmel, let's just try to remember where we are, okay.
Let's just try to remember why we're here.

CARMEL. You say you know me inside out. You don't know
anything. I could be a real dirty little slapper in my own
head, I could have a rich array of debased desires that would
blow your tiny mind.

JOE. Well, that's your own business and I respect that.

CARMEL. I don't want you to respect it. Fuck respecting it. I
want you to give a damn. I told you about that thing with the
Nigerian taxi driver.

JOE. What – thing with the Nigerian taxi driver?

CARMEL. I told you.

JOE. You told me you got a lift home from a Nigerian taxi
driver and you had a chat and he was nice.

CARMEL. Yes, he was. Very nice.

JOE. So what? You wanted to have sex with him, is that what
you're telling me?

CARMEL. Well.

JOE. Carmel, this *really* isn't appropriate /

CARMEL. I fell. On O'Connell Street and hurt my ankle. It
was after work and it was raining and I was there with a load
of bags and I slipped. And this very nice Nigerian fellow
driving a taxi saw, and he pulled in and got out and he was
very concerned. He insisted on having a look at my foot.

JOE. That's great.

CARMEL. I didn't want him to, because I didn't want the fuss,
but he was adamant. He made me sit in the back seat.

JOE. Carmel /

CARMEL. He took off my shoe and he took my ankle and –
very gently – he rotated it left and right the way they do at
the doctors'. And I noticed his hands were a bit rough.
Rougher than yours, but warm too.

JOE. Okay /

CARMEL. And I liked that. I really liked that. And as he was doing it I felt something, Joe. I felt something in the pit of my stomach – something I haven't felt for years.

JOE. I get it.

CARMEL. So I took a lift home with him. And we chatted. And he was very attentive and interested and caring. And it occurred to me that I have never had a lover like him. From a hot country, where jungles mix with cities and people sweat. Because our generation are not as well travelled as Emer's and our experiences are limited. And I thought – if I weren't married or if I was a different sort of person, it would be so easy at the end of this taxi ride to just – put my hand on his thigh and maybe move it up. And up. And up. And up and then just lean over and… ask him in.

Silence.

He looks at her aghast.

JOE. And what am I supposed to say to that?

CARMEL. Well, what do you think about it?

JOE. I think it's a bit racist to be honest.

CARMEL. Oh, for God's sake /

JOE. I do.

CARMEL. He was a nice, attractive man. I liked the colour of his skin, it was different to mine – that does not make me racist.

JOE. You're objectifying him.

CARMEL. I'm showing you what it is to get inside a person's head. It's called intimacy.

JOE. Well, I don't like it.

CARMEL. Surprise, surprise. There are things we don't know about each other, Joe.

JOE. So what? Why all of a sudden does everybody have to know everything about each other? When did we decide that unless we divulge every tiny detail of every stupid thought that we have, every minute of the day, that we're not living a proper life? When did that become love?

CARMEL. Honesty is important.

JOE. Is it?

CARMEL. It's all we have.

JOE. Are you glad you know my mother didn't like you working?

CARMEL. That's different.

JOE. Are you glad you know she thought your legs were fat?

CARMEL. She said heavy.

JOE. But are you glad you know it? Cos I'm not that glad I know that my daughter is entering wet T-shirt competitions on the other side of the world or that you're being felt up by taxi drivers and enjoying it. I'm not sure that all that knowledge will help me sleep easy at night. What happened to privacy? What happened to discretion? What happened to keeping it to yourself? Maybe there are some things we are better off not knowing. Maybe we can love each other despite.

CARMEL. I want to know my husband.

JOE. You do know your husband.

CARMEL. I want you to know me.

JOE. Look, Carmel – my mother was a mystery to me my whole frigging life. Did she love me? Did she hate me? How did she spend her afternoons?

CARMEL. That is not –

JOE. I'll never know the answers to those questions, Carmel. And you know what – I don't mind. I just want to bury the woman with a bit of dignity and get on with the rest of my life.

CARMEL. And what if I don't want to bury things? What then, Joe? Where do we go from there?

JOE. I can hear a car.

He runs to the door and looks out.

Yep. There's people coming. That's it – it's kicking off. Quickly, where are the stockings?

CARMEL *looks at him, then at the stockings in her hand.*

Carmel, come on – we can't have those things lying around. Give them to me or put them away.

He puts out his hand. CARMEL *still doesn't move.*

Carmel, for God's sake, there's people coming in here.

Slowly CARMEL *moves towards the coffin. She looks at the body.*

She then reaches down and opens the lapel on the jacket.

What the hell are you – Carmel, stop it.

She stuffs the stockings inside the corpse's jacket.

JOE *moves towards her but hesitates.*

He moves back to the door in case someone comes in.

Carmel – get a hold of yourself. Jesus. Take those out this minute. Do you hear me? Carmel. Carmel. *Carmel.* That's my mother.

CARMEL *smoothes the jacket down.* JOE *watches helplessly.*

The sense that people are about to arrive.

CARMEL *stands back and surveys the body.*

CARMEL. I think she looks perfect.

Beat.

She just never should have said my legs were fat.

Blackout.

THREE

The main living area of a small, somewhat neglected cottage in the wilds of West Cork.

Evening. As darkness approaches.

JOHNNY *and* MICHAEL *are holding* PEG *up, as they ease her into a wheelchair.* PEG *is resistant.*

PEG. I don't like this /

MICHAEL. We're nearly there, Ma. Have you got her, Johnny?

JOHNNY. Yeah.

MICHAEL. Sure?

JOHNNY. Yep.

MICHAEL. Now, when I give the word you just ease her down, alright.

PEG. I don't want / this.

JOHNNY. Okay /

MICHAEL. You ready?

JOHNNY. Yeah.

MICHAEL. Good man, now /

PEG. Please /

MICHAEL. On the count of three.

PEG. I can't /

MICHAEL. It's alright, Ma, we've got you. One, / two.

PEG. I'm going to fall /

JOHNNY. Ow.

MICHAEL. Keep hold of her, Johnny – three. There. Now.

We're done. She's down.

PEG *sits in the wheelchair, blinking at the boys.*

MICHAEL *pats* JOHNNY*'s shoulder.*

Good work. Johnny.

Beat.

(*To* PEG.) Now. Look at you there. All set. Isn't this great?

Everything about PEG*'s demeanor says it isn't.*

This thing's state-of-the-art you know. It's one of the best you can get. Folds up and everything – you can put it in the car, on the bus. We can bring it with us on drives if we want. When you're in Dublin. That'll be great, won't it? You can wheel yourself around the Phoenix Park. How do you feel?

PEG. Glorious. Like Aphrodite sprung from the shell.

MICHAEL. Ma, come on. This cost a lot of money.

PEG. I didn't tell you to buy it.

MICHAEL. No, I know you didn't, but – you won't know yourself when you get used to it, you really won't.

PEG. How much did you pay for it?

MICHAEL. It doesn't matter how much I paid. It's a present.

PEG *looks at the joystick on the handle of the wheelchair.*

PEG. What's this?

MICHAEL. That's to help you drive the thing. It's like a gear-stick. You just move it in whatever direction you want and off you go.

PEG *pushes the stick forward and drives straight at* MICHAEL. *She stops before she hits him.*

Jesus, Ma – careful with that.

PEG. I don't like this.

MICHAEL. You'll get used to it.

PEG. It's dangerous.

MICHAEL. It's not dangerous, it'll change your life. Think of the relief for your legs.

PEG. There's nothing wrong with my legs.

MICHAEL. That's not what the doctor said.

PEG. I walk up and down that hill every day.

MICHAEL. You don't have to use it every day. They just said they prefer people to have wheelchairs when they come in. Just in case.

PEG. Just in case what?

MICHAEL *looks at* JOHNNY.

MICHAEL. Just relax for a minute and get used to it. I'm going to finish with these (*Re: the boxes*.) – I reckon we'll have this place packed up in no time. Then we can treat ourselves to some fish and chips, what? You've been looking forward to that, haven't you, Johnny?

JOHNNY *doesn't say anything*.

MICHAEL *picks up a few boxes*. JOHNNY *starts to play with his PSP*.

PEG. I want to get out.

MICHAEL. Give it five minutes.

PEG. I don't want you spending your hard-earned money on things like this.

MICHAEL. It's a present, Ma.

PEG. Take it back to the shop.

MICHAEL. I can't take it back to the shop.

PEG. Why not?

MICHAEL. Because you need it. (*To* JOHNNY.) Here, you. Did I not say you're to put that thing away? How often do you see your grandmother? You're to talk to her when I'm outside. Help her get used to her wheelchair. Show her how to use that stick. If I see your nose stuck in that fecking thing one more time, I swear to God – Hey, Johnny? Do you hear me?

JOHNNY *nods.*

We're nearly there. Don't you start fading on me at the final hurdle.

MICHAEL *goes out with the box.*

PEG *moves the joystick and turns herself around in a circle in her wheelchair.*

She stops. She looks at JOHNNY.

PEG. People drop like flies in these places, you know.

Beat.

You know what I'm talking about. Don't pretend you don't.

Beat.

Perfectly healthy men and women, whose only crime is getting on a bit – snatched from their houses by well-meaning relatives and brought to these – places. These – homes – that's a euphemism if ever I heard one. They go in there able as you like. Nothing more wrong with them than a wobbly pair of knees and bad eyesight. Three months later – gone. Just like that. And do you know why?

JOHNNY *shakes his head.*

Rat poison. The nurses put it in the mashed potatoes. Not much, mind you. Maybe just a pinch, between the thumb and forefinger. Just enough you mightn't even notice anything, except that maybe your food tasted a bit more peppery than normal. But one pinch of that stuff every day and soon enough you're looking at full-blown organ failure. Heart, kidneys, liver, all slowly melting as the months pass by. And no one is the wiser. Natural causes they say – to comfort the families, but let me tell you, Johnny – there are no natural causes in this life. Not that anyone'd notice in one of these places. Room upon room of dopey silver-haired relics lying in bed with bits of tubes sticking out of them and eyes like saucers. The nurses probably think they're putting them out of their misery. But I'm not in misery, Johnny. I'm not in misery here. This is my castle. My Camelot... Have you ever seen a dead body before?

JOHNNY *shakes his head.*

How old are you now?

JOHNNY. Twelve.

PEG. I suppose they'd keep you away from that sort of thing at twelve. Unless it was a close relative. Unless it was me. They'd probably let you come and see me if I was dead so's you could bid your last farewells. Don't you think?

He shrugs.

Can you imagine, Johnny, what that would be like? Coming to see me. And I'm dead. Think about that there for a moment. Imagine my face all grey and ashen and my mouth hanging open at the side like this. Bits of white crust hardened on my lip. Can you imagine having to see that? And knowing, knowing all along that it's the rat poison that got me and that if I'd been left in my own house in the country, the pink would still be in my cheeks and the light in my eyes? (*She begins to wheel herself towards him.*) Think about that there for a moment, Johnny. Think about looking into my dead cold eyes and face. Think about touching my skin and giving me a kiss goodbye on my forehead. They'll make you do that, Johnny. They will. And let me tell you, you have never in your life felt anything like the cold of a corpse.

She stops the chair in front of him. They look at each other.

I'll pay you if you help me get out of this chair.

MICHAEL *comes back in.*

MICHAEL. See you're getting a feel for it now, aren't you? Only takes a bit of practice.

PEG. And I'll have plenty of time to practise up in Dublin, I suppose. With all that time on my hands.

MICHAEL *chooses to ignore her.*

MICHAEL. You've some new neighbours up on the hill I see.

PEG. They're Germans.

MICHAEL. Are they?

PEG. Well-meaning ones. They've turned the McCarthys' old place into a yoga centre. With incense and Buddha statues and pictures of gurus. The Yanks love it.

MICHAEL. Well, they're having a bonfire of some sort.

PEG. That's because it's a full moon. They have a drumming circle if it's a full moon.

MICHAEL. Well, that's nice and normal, isn't it?

PEG. They're spiritual.

MICHAEL. Of course they are.

PEG. She's a very nice lady, Brigitta. Never wears a bra. She gives me lifts into town sometimes. Helps me carry the shopping. She came over here for a cup of tea one day and showed me an exercise called 'The Cobra'. Right there on the floor.

MICHAEL. 'The Cobra'?

PEG. It's not as filthy as it sounds. It's for your spine. We could call in on them if you want. Say hello.

MICHAEL. No thanks.

PEG. She's about your age, Brigitta. No visible husband. I wouldn't say she's beautiful now but she's certainly got flexibility and that's got to count for something.

MICHAEL *picks up another box.*

MICHAEL. Don't think we're going to have time for house calls tonight, Ma.

PEG. What do you mean – not have time?

MICHAEL. It's a four-hour drive.

PEG. We're not leaving till morning. Brigitta's my neighbour. I can't go without saying goodbye. She's been good to me.

MICHAEL. You can't say goodbye to everyone, Ma. We'll be here all week at that rate.

In his back pocket, MICHAEL*'s phone goes. He can't answer.*

Ah – here. Grab that for me, will you, Johnny?

JOHNNY *retrieves the phone from* MICHAEL*'s pocket.*

PEG. Brigitta has one of those new phones too.

MICHAEL. Does she? Who is it, Johnny?

JOHNNY *looks at him.*

I don't fucking believe this. It couldn't be.

JOHNNY *nods.*

Jesus Christ, that's the second time in an hour. She's certifiable you know that. She's fucking loop-the-loop. Someone should sit her down and examine her goddam head.

JOHNNY *nods.*

Well, go on and answer it before she goes and calls the police or something. Fuck's sake.

JOHNNY *answers the phone and holds it up to* MICHAEL*'s ear. Balancing it precariously between shoulder and ear,* MICHAEL *leaves.*

Hello? Yeah… Did I not say I'd call you back at seven? Well, it's not seven.

PEG *leans towards* JOHNNY.

PEG. There's a ten-euro note in my bag. It's yours if you help me out of this thing.

JOHNNY *shakes his head.*

I'll let you play your game.

JOHNNY *shakes his head.*

I promise.

JOHNNY. He said not to.

PEG. Who? Him? He's not the boss. I'm the boss around here. This is my house. If you want to play your game, play your game. I'm the boss and I say you can play your game. Go on. Play your game. Play your game, Johnny. Play your game. Play your game. I'm the boss here. Me.

He doesn't move.

She looks at JOHNNY – *a sense of defeat.*

No. No. I suppose that's – a fair point. Now that you say it.

She puts her hands in her lap and looks around.

Well. He says this place is somewhere on the Southside.
Near the sea. That's another of their tricks, of course. To lure
you. They say things like: 'It's near the sea, there'll be tea
and sandwiches and board games. It'll be just like Brittas
Bay.' And then out they come with their boxes of poison and
their death warrants. I'm no fool. I know what it's going to
be like. And Dublin's a grey place. Never liked Dublin
people. Cold. Cold sorts.

Beat.

How's your mother?

JOHNNY. Fine.

PEG. She's from Dublin. But she has a lovely long neck which
is her redemption. She's got a new job, I hear. In an office.

JOHNNY *nods.*

And a new boyfriend?

JOHNNY. Yeah.

PEG. Owns the office, does he?

JOHNNY *shrugs.*

Have you met him?

JOHNNY *nods.*

Is he nice?

JOHNNY *shakes his head.*

No?

JOHNNY *shakes his head.*

Is he not handsome?

JOHNNY. He looks like a pig.

PEG. I see.

JOHNNY (*passionately*). He's no hair on his head but loads in his nose. And his teeth are yellow with brown at the sides and his belly's like a big sack full of shite.

PEG. Well. That's a very powerful description. I've a clear visual image of the man now. Thank you, Johnny. God love your poor mother putting up with that for the sake of a bit of warmth beside her.

Beat.

You've an imagination, I see. Hang on to that. A rich interior life is a great liberation. Of course, the wrong kind of interior life can be a prison of its own making. Your grandfather knew all about that. He broke my nose, you know. Twice.

MICHAEL *can be heard approaching the door. He's still on the phone.*

MICHAEL. I know… Yeah, I *get* that – what did I just say to you – he'll be home well before… Yes, I hear – *I hear you, okay?*… I'm not raising my – I am not raising my – I am *not*… oh, look, fuck this – here. Talk to your son.

MICHAEL *thrusts the phone at* JOHNNY.

It's your mother. Tell her you're grand.

JOHNNY *takes the phone.* MICHAEL *stands over him listening, tense.*

JOHNNY. Hello?… Fine… Yeah… Just Granny… Fine… Fish and chips… Fine… 'kay bye.

He hangs up and hands the phone to MICHAEL *who looks at him in disbelief.*

MICHAEL. Is that it?

JOHNNY *looks at him.*

That's all you're going to say? 'Yes, fine, fish and fucking chips.' Jesus, Johnny, she'll be up the friggin' walls now, thinking I've got you held hostage here. Thinking I've got you muzzled. Why didn't you tell her what we're doing?

JOHNNY. I did.

MICHAEL. Why didn't you tell her we were having a nice time?

JOHNNY. I did /

MICHAEL. Here with Granny. Helping Granny move.

JOHNNY. She knows.

MICHAEL. She does not know. She'll be up to ninety now.

PEG. Leave him, Michael.

MICHAEL. You've no idea what she's like. You don't know the grief. Barely lets him off the leash for a second. Takes him to endless doctors and nutritionists and God knows what. He's got ADD now – that's the fucking latest. She's all worked up, giving him pills, not letting him have sausages, when the fact is it's probably because he's got his head stuck in fucking computer games twenty-four-seven and his mother's a nutcase. It's her that's the problem. Her.

PEG. You know who you sound like now.

MICHAEL. Here, give me that fecking thing in your pocket.

JOHNNY. What?

MICHAEL. Give it to me.

JOHNNY. No.

MICHAEL. Give it to me, Johnny. Now.

PEG. Leave him alone, Michael.

MICHAEL. That's the cause of all this. That's why his brain is fucking fried. I said give it here.

MICHAEL *grabs* JOHNNY *and pulls the PSP violently out of his pocket.*

JOHNNY. Ow. You're hurting.

MICHAEL. I don't care, I'm sick of looking at the thing. I want a human being for a son, not a bloody zombie. You should've said we were having a nice time together – you should have said that we'd had a nice drive and I'd bought you a good lunch and you were enjoying your dad – and your grandmother's company. You should have told her that. Would that have been too much to bloody ask?

PEG. That tone could be your father now /

MICHAEL. Well, you know, Ma, maybe he had a point. Maybe he was tired of working his bollix off all the time and no one giving a shite. That would make anyone angry. That would make anyone feel like lashing out.

JOHNNY. They put rat poison in the food.

MICHAEL. What?

JOHNNY. The nurses.

MICHAEL. What nurses? What are you talking about now?

JOHNNY. In the place where Granny's going. They put rat poison in the food.

MICHAEL. Rat poison? Where did you – were you filling his head up with nonsense?

JOHNNY. It melts your organs.

MICHAEL. What? Jesus Christ, Ma. What have you been saying?

PEG. I know what goes on in these places.

MICHAEL. You can't fill a kid's head with stuff like that. He's a kid. The last thing I need is her on the blower saying he's been wetting the bed again cos you've been scaring the shite out of him.

PEG. Does he wet the bed?

JOHNNY. No.

MICHAEL. There is no rat poison in the place where Granny's going, alright. It's a home for the elderly. It's got a garden and televisions and the staff are lovely.

PEG. All serial killers have charm.

MICHAEL. Jesus, Ma, I'm killing myself with all this. If I had wanted to poison you I could have done it myself and used the money to go to Tenerife.

PEG. You need a woman.

MICHAEL. Don't start that again.

PEG. You need a bit of softness in your life.

MICHAEL. And I'll get that from a woman, will I? Fat fucking chance.

PEG. What happened to that lady doctor you liked?

MICHAEL. I didn't like her.

PEG. You were always talking about her.

MICHAEL. No I wasn't.

PEG. You were.

MICHAEL. She's a friend.

PEG. Well, that's a good start.

MICHAEL. She's a lesbian, Ma, alright. She's not interested in men.

MICHAEL *picks up another box.*

I can't take much more of this.

PEG. A lesbian?

MICHAEL. Yes, Ma. A lesbian.

PEG. But you took her to dinner.

MICHAEL. I know.

PEG. Was she always a lesbian?

MICHAEL. I don't know, Ma, but while you're chewing on that, I think you should know, we're going to have to leave tonight.

PEG. What?

MICHAEL. Once I've brought these outside.

PEG. We can't leave tonight. You said /

MICHAEL. I know what I said. But it's not up to me. Nothing, it seems, is up to me any more.

PEG. But /

MICHAEL. She wants him home tonight for some martial-arts thing she's booked him into tomorrow morning and despite the fact it's my weekend with him and I told her we were here till Sunday and I've already paid for the B&B, she's insisting on having her way.

PEG. But I'm not /

MICHAEL. I'm not arguing any more, Ma. I'm done arguing with her. Like all women she always gets what she wants in the end. Johnny, grab the door for me.

He leaves.

PEG *looks at* JOHNNY.

PEG. I'd like to meet these women he's talking about. Who are always getting what they want in the end.

JOHNNY *puts his hands in his pocket.*

I'm disappointed about the doctor. I was sure he had a gra for her. His voice relaxed when he talked about her. Did you notice?

JOHNNY *shrugs.*

Are there girls in your school, Johnny?

JOHNNY. Yeah.

PEG. Do you like any of them?

JOHNNY. They're okay.

PEG. Well, that's not much of a recommendation. Desire keeps the spirit alive. A great passion should be an all-consuming furnace tearing through your body like a forest fire. Making you shiver. Making you ache. There should be no respite from the exquisite longing it sends through your bones... Are there any girls in your class that stoke the longing in your bones, Johnny?

JOHNNY *shrugs.*

What about the boys?

Beat.

Do you like any of the boys, you know… the way you might like the girls?

JOHNNY. Get lost.

PEG. Nothing to be ashamed of if you did. You are who you are. The important thing is not to twist it down inside yourself so it comes out gnarled and rancid and aimed in every direction but your own.

Beat.

Your granddad liked boys.

JOHNNY *laughs*.

JOHNNY. Yeah right.

PEG. You never met him, of course, and if you had, you wouldn't have suspected it. But it was men alright. For him.

He had what you might call a military streak, your granddad. All that washing of himself until his skin was red and swollen and the way he polished his shoes twice a day with the rigour of a midwife. He had me starching the towels and bleaching the sheets so often I once got a rash on my arms and had to go the hospital for a cream. They thought I'd been in a fire.

Beat.

He used inspect the cupboards too, your granddad. And the drawers. And the pantry in the evenings to make sure the jars were all in order and the tins were lined up straight. And if there was so much as a fork that wasn't gleaming or a napkin not folded just so, well… you don't want to know what was in store for us. Your dad, when he was little, used to check the pantry every night before granddad got in, so's I wouldn't get the brunt of it. Your poor old dad doing that for his mother. It's no wonder his nerves have gone. We do terrible things to our children without realising it.

Beat.

Your grandfather was a very handsome man, you know. Like your own dad. Handsome men have a terrible burden on them. All that choice so early. All that promise. I was beside myself when he asked me to marry him. Broke my poor sister Annie's heart in accepting. Annie was madly in love with your granddad. They were the same age but he picked me because his best friend Jack Collins told him I was the most beautiful girl in Munster. And, I suppose, if you've no real feeling for women you have to go for the girl other men think is the most beautiful girl in Munster. What other way of judging have you got? He courted me so precisely before we married. Your grandfather. Took me to dances and films and concerts. I thought I was a queen – I thought I was going to have the life of... until my wedding night.

MICHAEL *comes back in*.

MICHAEL. That drumming circle's really heating up. Do they do this all the time?

PEG. Once every month.

MICHAEL (*glancing out the window*). They're not going to start taking their clothes off or anything, are they?

PEG. They might.

MICHAEL. Well, all I can say is the sooner we have you out of here the better. I don't like the idea of you stuck down in the middle of nowhere with a bunch of horny hippies.

PEG. The McCarthys that lived there before were worse.

MICHAEL. At least they acted like normal people. Would you look at your man there with the feather thing on his head?

PEG *wheels herself to the window*.

PEG. That's Ivan.

MICHAEL. Who's Ivan?

PEG. He's a shaman

MICHAEL. A shaman?

PEG. He works with the spirits – pulls invisible knives out of people's backs for forty euro.

MICHAEL. It's amazing the things people pay money for.

PEG. He trims hedges as well. Look at his arms. The women round here love him, but he doesn't believe in monogamy. I told Brigitta to stay away from him so. No matter how enlightened a man might appear, no one is immune to chlamydia.

MICHAEL. Ah, Ma.

PEG. There's no point sticking your head in the sand, Michael. I hope you're getting yourself tested with regularity.

MICHAEL. Stop it, Ma.

PEG. Which one is the brake?

MICHAEL. What do you want the brake for?

PEG. I want to know how to stop this if I have to go downhill. Here, I have it.

MICHAEL. See, you're flying it now. I told you it'd be fun. Johnny, go into the kitchen and grab us out the sweeping brush will you? Sure, we'll be finished in no time now.

JOHNNY *goes*.

MICHAEL *looks at* PEG.

Are you getting anything out of him?

PEG. Who?

MICHAEL. Johnny. Is he telling you anything?

PEG. About what?

MICHAEL. Anything. Four hours in the car on the drive down, he barely uttered two words. Four fucking hours. Got to me after a while – I found myself getting panicky with it. Had to turn up the radio. Is that normal, do you think, for twelve?

PEG. You were a quiet child.

MICHAEL. Well, we had to be.

PEG. He's alright.

MICHAEL. What's he saying?

PEG. I'm telling him about Granddad.

MICHAEL. Oh.

PEG. Do you remember that friend of his, Jack Collins?

MICHAEL. Is he the one who wouldn't wear shoelaces because they were made by capitalists?

PEG. The very one.

MICHAEL. Sort of. I remember him shuffling around in shoes that were too big for him and helping himself to Dad's whiskey. He'd been to the Crumlin Road, hadn't he? For trying to kill a British soldier.

PEG. That's right.

MICHAEL. That's mad. Dad hanging around with criminals.

PEG. Your father worshipped Jack.

MICHAEL. Why?

PEG. Because he did things.

MICHAEL. And Dad never did anything. He was a strange man.

PEG. He was.

MICHAEL. Here, you've not been frightening him, have you? About Dad.

PEG. He has no sense of family.

MICHAEL. Well, that's not my fault. I didn't tell you to move yourself down here to the arse-end of nowhere away from everyone. Anyway, once we get you back to Dublin, he'll have plenty of sense of family. We'll be in to see you every week. Every weekend.

JOHNNY *returns*.

That'll be great, won't it, Johnny? Visiting Granny every weekend up in Dublin.

PEG. He's beside himself with excitement.

MICHAEL. He is. Now. Look. You know the best way to sweep the floors, don't you, Johnny? Start with the corners like this and sweep the bits into a pile in the middle. Like that. Yeah?

PEG *tries to get out of her chair.*

PEG. I'll show him.

MICHAEL. No, no. You rest yourself, Ma. Johnny can do it, can't you, Johnny? Show me and Granny how you sweep the floors. Go on.

JOHNNY *takes the sweeping brush and tentatively begins to sweep.*

Good man. He's a good man, isn't he, Ma?

PEG. He's great.

MICHAEL. I used to have to do that every day for my father. He used to check to make sure I'd got up every last speck of dust.

PEG. I was telling him.

MICHAEL. Sure, I'm glad of it now. I'm the only single man I know who doesn't have a cleaner. Not bad in a recession, eh?

PEG. Let's go to America.

MICHAEL. Huh?

PEG. Let's go and see your sisters.

MICHAEL. What are you saying?

PEG. I haven't been to America for years. We could have an adventure. You'd like that, wouldn't you, Johnny?

JOHNNY. Yeah.

MICHAEL. We're having an adventure here. We're going to Dublin.

PEG. I want a different sort of adventure. I want to go to America. You should have stayed out there while you had the chance.

MICHAEL. I never had the chance. I worked there for one summer in a bar.

PEG. You should have stayed there like your sisters and married
an American woman. American women are very forward.
They wouldn't let a handsome man like you sit and stagnate.
They'd be flocking around you like crows to a rasher.

MICHAEL. I don't want women flocking around me like crows
to a rasher. I've enough trouble in my life.

PEG. Your sisters are happy out there.

MICHAEL. Yeah, I know. They're so happy there they never
come home. I don't see them down here worrying about you.
I don't see them lifting boxes and sweeping floors and
buying you wheelchairs. I don't see them busting a gut to
help you move.

PEG. I don't want them busting a gut to help me move. They
have their own lives. I don't want to move.

MICHAEL. You missed a bit there, Johnny.

PEG. I want to stay in my own house.

MICHAEL. Well, you know, Ma, I'd like a weekend free of
duty and obligation and orders – I *really* would but sometimes we just have to work with what life hands us and we'd
all be a lot better off if we were to do it with a bit of grace
instead of bitching and moaning all the time. (*He glances out
the window.*) Fucking hell, they are taking off their clothes.
Would you – Jesus. Johnny, avert your gaze.

PEG *wheels herself over to the window.*

PEG. Brigitta's the one with the red hair.

MICHAEL. Is she now?

PEG. What do you think of her?

MICHAEL. Well, it's sort of hard to see her under that sheet
she's waving.

PEG. Let's go and say hello.

MICHAEL *picks up a box.*

MICHAEL. I don't think they'll appreciate being interrupted. Johnny, you finish these floors for me and then the three of us can head off and get some food in our bellies. It's been a long old day. I think we're all suffering from low blood-sugar.

MICHAEL walks out with the box. PEG *watches* JOHNNY *sweeping.*

The faint sound of drumming.

PEG. Sounds like they're having a great old time up there, doesn't it?

JOHNNY *shrugs.*

You wouldn't like to be up there with them, dancing round the fire?

JOHNNY *shakes his head.* PEG *wheels herself in a circle and stops.*

Give me your hand.

JOHNNY *looks at her. He doesn't move.*

Your hand, Johnny.

Slowly JOHNNY *puts out his hand.* PEG *takes it.*

She clutches it to her for a second, tightly.

She lets it go.

JOHNNY *starts sweeping again.*

Annie, my sister, lent me her stockings once. Which I suppose means she forgave me for marrying your granddad. People probably think two sisters sharing stockings is unhygienic nowadays but in those times we all did it. As long as you didn't put a tear in them and hand-washed them before you gave them back. They were lovely silken ones with a seam up the back that she'd gotten from London. I suppose they were a bit racy for the time but I was a married girl. Married a whole year at that point. I thought he'd like silk stockings.

We were still living in Cork at the time, but we decided to take a trip up to Dublin, to see a jazz singer that your

granddad's friend Jack Collins got us tickets to. And me and
your granddad and Jack had booked to stay overnight in a
hotel. People didn't do things like that much back then, it
was very extravagant. I'd had my hair done and had bought a
new skirt and I knew I looked great because Jack kept telling
me I was gorgeous and we had drinks bought for us by a
group of strangers at the next table who said we were bright
young things. And the jazz singer was a curvaceous creature
in a red silk dress whose voice cradled and caressed and
wrapped itself around us – until the whole room was
throbbing with exhilaration at the sheer luck of being alive.

And still, the only thing I could think about that night was
getting back to the hotel room with your granddad and
showing him how I'd learned to take off my stockings in a
way that men were supposed to respond to. I'd practised with
Annie. You had to turn your foot a certain direction and lift
your leg up high so – well, you don't need to know the details
but it was very compelling stuff… in any case I never got to
show your granddad what I'd learned because no sooner had
we left Jack and our new friends at the next table and got
inside our room – but he belted me straight in the face with
his fist. I got blood all over the lovely floral eiderdown.

Beat.

And on the carpet, which was green. And on Annie's
stockings which I washed at four o'clock in the morning in
the hotel sink. My eyes stinging, but I wanted them clean.
We left early the next day. I didn't want Jack Collins to see
my face and neither did your grandfather and the doctor said
I was very unlucky to have fallen on the stairs in such a
manner because I'd gone and broken my nose. Couldn't
bring myself to give Annie back her stockings after that.
Even though I'd got the blood out. I didn't want my sister
going out in them and catching all that… pain. So I lied and
said I lost them.

JOHNNY *looks at her.*

I don't think she ever forgave me for that one.

She looks around the room. She sees her handbag.

Would you bring me that little bag there by the window, Johnny? There's a bit of old blushing powder in it somewhere. Jack Collins used say a woman should always have a bit of a flush in her cheeks.

JOHNNY *brings her the bag.*

She rummages through it and takes out some blusher and puts it on her face.

What do they teach you in school, Johnny?

JOHNNY *shrugs.*

Do you know who Cú Chulainn is?

He nods.

Do you study the myths at all? You know, stories about men who were like gods and gods who were like men. And women.

He doesn't respond.

The unquenchable Queen Medb – do you know her?

He shakes his head.

What about the Ancient Greeks?

He shrugs, keeps sweeping. She goes back to her face.

The Ancient Greeks liked women to be pale. They were always praising white-skinned beauties. Hera the Queen of the gods whose husband Zeus was a desperate womaniser. Helen of Troy, her sister Clytemnestra who was killed by her own son in the end. There were a lot of pale, unhappy ladies in Ancient Greece, Johnny. But just because you have a tragic life doesn't mean you have to have a tragic story. We make our own stories. We're none of us gods, but we've that.

She takes out a small compact mirror, looks at herself.

Jack Collins wouldn't have agreed with the Greeks. About the pale skin. He had a book with pictures of women – from places like India and South America – in saris and headscarves and baring their breasts. He used show me that book sometimes.

She continues to apply make-up – lipstick, perfume, whatever.

I ran away with Jack Collins. Just the once.

He called to the house one Sunday afternoon and asked me to go for a drive. The children were over at Annie's, so I had a few hours to spare. We were on the road so long that it started to get dark. So we found a room in a place in the countryside where the woman didn't ask us any questions because I was wearing a wedding ring. And Jack – Jack said he wanted to take me away with him and look after me the way a woman should be looked after and I said he could, but I knew that he couldn't because I had three children and a house and a husband. And anyway, no man, no matter how much he loves the curve of a woman's belly, can ever really look after her. But I said it because it fitted the occasion. And the next morning myself and Jack Collins drove home in the same clothes we'd worn the day before and your grandfather didn't ask me where I'd been and I didn't say. And Jack – Jack went to Europe a few weeks after that. Married an East German girl… He never said goodbye to either one of us.

PEG *looks at* JOHNNY. *She holds some eyeshadow out towards him.*

Will you put a bit of this around my eyes for me?

He hesitates.

JOHNNY. I don't know how.

PEG. It's just like colouring-in. Don't go over the lines. Here, give me that sweeping brush so you've your hands free.

JOHNNY *hands* PEG *the sweeping brush and tentatively begins to apply eyeshadow with his finger to* PEG's *face.*

MICHAEL *comes to the doorway. He watches them.*

MICHAEL. What's going on here?

PEG. Johnny's just helping me put on my face.

MICHAEL. Is he now? Who are you trying to impress?

PEG. I've no one left to impress.

MICHAEL. Are those floors finished?

JOHNNY goes to take the sweeping brush but PEG hangs onto it.

PEG. They'll do.

MICHAEL. There'll be no room for the rest of us if we put any more boxes into that van.

PEG. So what are we going to do?

MICHAEL. I think we should call it a day and hit the road.

PEG. But what about my things?

MICHAEL. You'll have your things. I'll just have to drive back down next weekend and collect them.

PEG. Really? You'd do that?

MICHAEL. Of course I would. I don't have a choice.

PEG. So I can stay here till next week?

MICHAEL. No, Ma. You're coming back with us now.

PEG. But I won't have my things.

MICHAEL. They're expecting you tomorrow. The room's all ready. Everyone's looking forward to meeting you.

He opens a box and pulls out a jug.

I mean, are you going to die without this for one week? I don't think so. Come on, let's head down to the village and get some food and give ourselves a pat on the back for a job well done.

PEG. I want to say goodbye to Brigitta.

MICHAEL *looks out the window.*

MICHAEL. Brigitta's otherwise engaged.

PEG. Well then, I'll say goodbye in the morning.

MICHAEL. Come on, Ma, give me a break. We're going to go down to the village and have some fish and chips and you can have a cold gin and tonic and then you'll feel better.

PEG. I feel fine.

MICHAEL *stands behind the wheelchair and tries to push it. It doesn't move.*

MICHAEL. We're all hungry and a bit cranky but once we've some food inside us… Fuck, what's wrong with this thing?

PEG. How much are you planning to get for this place?

MICHAEL. What?

PEG. Because if it's money you're after I can get you money.

MICHAEL. From where exactly? Jesus, Johnny, can you work this?

JOHNNY *and* MICHAEL *try to push the wheelchair but it stays firmly rooted to the ground.*

PEG. Are you going to sell it? Is that the plan?

MICHAEL. There is no plan yet, Ma.

PEG. Rent it out to a bunch of American tourists to practise their headstands in.

MICHAEL. That's not a bad idea, you know.

PEG. This is my house.

MICHAEL. I'm joking, Ma.

PEG. I want to know what you are going to do with it.

MICHAEL. I haven't decided what I'm going to do with it. It's not a great time out there – you might have heard. No one knows what'll happen tomorrow.

PEG. No one ever knows what'll happen tomorrow.

MICHAEL. You're not safe here, Ma. Have you got your hands on the brake. Is that what it is?

PEG. Only thing I ever got for myself was this cottage.

MICHAEL. Ma /

PEG. I fell in love with this cottage the moment I saw it.

MICHAEL. I know /

PEG. I'd never even paid a bill myself before your father died but after he went –

MICHAEL. After he went you found your independence, I know, Ma. You've told me. Though I might remind you that you only found that independence through his civil service pension and his savings so it's not quite the feminist triumph you have it marked out as.

PEG. I never said it was a triumph. Freedom is supposed to be a right.

Beat.

I can sing in this cottage at the top of my voice. I can smash every plate in the kitchen if I want to. I can paint the walls purple /

MICHAEL. Listen /

PEG. And there's no one here to say I can't. When I saw this cottage I knew it was a place I could be myself.

MICHAEL. And you've been yourself.

PEG. 'Been'?

MICHAEL *gets up, forceful.*

MICHAEL. It's not going to happen, Ma. It's not possible, alright? I can't have an eighty-year-old woman down here in some little house, in the middle of nowhere, on her own. I can't have you living in a place – where if you fall, or hurt yourself or break your hip – or – or — anything happens, no one will know. I can't have that. It isn't right and it isn't fair. I can't sleep at night for all the fucking things I have to think about and I can't be thinking about this. You're coming to Dublin tonight and that's it. Now stop digging your – wheels in and let me move this thing.

They look at each other. There is a stalemate.

Right. I'll lift you up out of this if I have to.

MICHAEL *moves around to lift her out of the wheelchair.*

She picks up the sweeping brush and hits him with it.

PEG. Don't come near me.

MICHAEL. Ma, Jesus.

He tries to duck around her. She hits him again.

Ma!

PEG. I want to stay in my house /

She starts thrashing him with the brush.

MICHAEL. Ma, come on /

PEG. I want to say goodbye to Brigitta.

MICHAEL. Would you stop it?

PEG. I want to say goodbye to my friends /

MICHAEL. Stop it.

PEG. You can't make me leave.

MICHAEL. Ma, put down the goddam sweeping brush /

PEG. You can't make me go /

MICHAEL. This is ridiculous, Ma /

She thrashes harder. Wildly.

PEG. You don't know me.

MICHAEL. Ma –

PEG. I'm not ready /

MICHAEL. Ow. Please. Jesus /

PEG. I'm not ready. I'm not ready. I'm not ready. I'M NOT READY TO GO.

She throws the brush at him and sits in the chair, exhausted.

MICHAEL *stands, not quite knowing what to do.*

MICHAEL. Ma. Please. For – for God's sake…

Silence. `

I'm – I'm just trying to do my best here. I'm just trying to. You can't stay here, Ma. You know that. You can't… I mean – what… what… what do you want me to do?

She sits up and looks at him.

PEG. I want you to make a grand gesture.

MICHAEL. A grand – gesture?

PEG. I want you to go up to the hill and introduce yourself to Brigitta.

MICHAEL. Ma, that's – I'm not. No. I'm not doing that.

PEG. I want you to introduce yourself to Brigitta, as my handsome son, and tell her you're taking me away and I'm not going to be back.

MICHAEL. Now look –

PEG. And I'd like you to be elegant and remember your manners. And stay up there and listen to them drumming and have a drink and a laugh and show them your son.

MICHAEL. Ma –

PEG. That's what I want you to do, Michael. I want you to go up there and do that so that I can sit here and say goodbye by myself.

MICHAEL. But /

PEG. You asked me and I told you.

MICHAEL. I don't want to go up there, Ma.

PEG. There'll be food, Brigitta's a great cook.

MICHAEL. Brigitta's mental. Brigitta doesn't even have a top on right now. I don't want to go and listen to drumming. I've spent the whole day breaking my back for /

PEG. Sometimes we do things we don't want to.

MICHAEL. I know, Ma. That's what I've been telling you.

PEG. I made your father a cup of tea and rubbed the back of his head the night we heard Jack Collins had left for Germany. Not because I wanted to. Not because the man treated me with any kindness or tenderness or respect. Not because I wouldn't have loved to have gathered the three of you in my arms and taken us all as far away from him as we could get so's we

could have ourselves some peace. No. I did it because I knew
his battered heart was broken at losing the love of his life. And
even I could have some sympathy for that.

MICHAEL. Look, Ma.

PEG. Go.

He looks at her.

Please.

Beat.

Please.

Beat.

Please.

Beat.

Please, Michael.

MICHAEL. ...Come on, Johnny. We'll head up to the hippies
so, but we're only going to stay for half an hour. And then
we're leaving and I mean it. No more of this nonsense, Ma.
When we come back you're getting in the car and I don't
want to hear another word about it.

She nods.

Okay?

She looks at him.

PEG. Okay.

MICHAEL. Let's go, Johnny.

JOHNNY *heads out,* MICHAEL *turns back.*

You're not... going to do anything – stupid while we're
gone, are you?

She shakes her head.

Promise?

She nods.

Good.

MICHAEL *leaves. Offstage we hear him say:*

Come here, what was she saying about Dad and Jack Collins?

PEG *sits in the wheelchair as they move away. The drumming is sounding faintly, off.*

Very gently, she tries to pull herself out of the chair and stand up but the effort gets the better of her.

She looks at the gearstick and slowly wheels herself towards one of the few remaining boxes.

She leans forward and reaches inside it and takes out a half-drunk bottle of sherry and a small glass, followed by a leather case. She places the objects on her knee and wheels herself back to the centre of the room. She finds a place to rest the glass and pours herself a drink.

Then she unzips the leather case and from it retrieves a pair of silk stockings. She unravels them one at a time in her hands before laying them carefully on the table.

She goes back to the leather case and lastly takes out a pristine white Apple MacBook.

She puts it on the table, opens it and turns it on.

As the start-up music sounds, PEG *pushes herself out of the chair with great effort until finally she is standing on both feet. She takes one of the stockings off the table, and shaky but with great determination, bends down towards her foot.*

She carefully rolls the stocking onto her foot and, with a sudden elegant flourish we have not seen before, continues rolling it up her leg.

When she has finished she does exactly the same thing with the other stocking. The lights very slowly begin to dim around her, the drumming becoming a little louder.

When she has both stockings on, she studies her legs for a beat before slowly lowering her skirt and gently sitting herself back down into the wheelchair. She takes a sip of her drink, closes her eyes for a beat and takes a deep breath.

The lights continue to dim.

She opens her eyes again, turns towards the computer and begins to type. She types and types, the drumming a faint heartbeat all around her as the lights move to black.

The End.

A Nick Hern Book

No Romance first published in Great Britain in 2011 as a paperback original by Nick Hern Books Limited, 14 Larden Road, London W3 7ST in association with the Abbey Theatre

No Romance copyright © 2011 Nancy Harris

Nancy Harris has asserted her right to be identified as the author of this work

Cover image by Adriana Campuzano
Cover design by Ned Hoste

Typeset by Nick Hern Books
Printed in the UK by CLE Print Ltd, St Ives, Cambs, PE27 3LE

A CIP catalogue record for this book is available from the British Library

ISBN 978 1 84842 161 5